# The New Divorce Paradigm

## Transitioning Your Relationship with Integrity

Moreah Ragusa

Published by:
The Phoenix Coaching and Transformation Corporation
11550 - 44 Street SE, Calgary, Alberta, Canada  T2Z 4A2

Copyright © 2006 Moreah Ragusa
First Printing, November 2006
Printed in Canada

Cover design, text layout, and graphics by Shelley Hedges
Edited by Simone Gabbay
Author photo by Carolyn Sandstrom

Library and Archives Canada Cataloguing in Publication

Ragusa, Moreah
        The New Divorce Paradigm: Transitioning  Your
Relationship with Integrity / Moreah Ragusa.

ISBN 0-9781145-1-5

1. Psychology.  2. Relationship.  3. Self-Help.  I. Title.

Inquiries, orders, and other requests should be addressed to:
The Phoenix Coaching and Transformation Corporation
11550 - 44 Street SE, Calgary, Alberta, Canada  T2Z 4A2
Phone 403-278-3700
E-mail: info@thephoenixcoaching.com

www.thephoenixcoaching.com

May the powerful journey of divorce
awaken within you
long-dormant forces of wisdom and insight
to help you establish a new life
with love and integrity.

With Gratitude and Love,
Moreah

The *Integrity Divorce* symbol depicted on the cover
and at chapter beginnings represents the souls'
completeness, separate but forever connected,
as explored in *The New Divorce Paradigm.*

# Table of Contents

# Table of Contents

## The New Divorce Paradigm

---

The New Divorce Paradigm
represents truthfulness, empowerment, and
equality in the divorce process.
It is founded upon the desire to act with
integrity in the completion of a sacred union
shared between two people.
The 12 Integrity Divorce Principles™,
which are outlined in the pages
following the Introduction, are the mandates
and building blocks for achieving
the New Divorce Paradigm.

---

# The Power of Forgiveness

As a longtime student and teacher of the spiritual self-study text *A Course in Miracles* (ACIM), I believe that I attracted into my life the opportunities to free myself from deeply seated unconscious guilt that was imbedded within *a part of my mind*. The guilt I speak of is actually within a part of most of our minds (excluding only the minds of fully enlightened masters) and is derived from a mistaken belief that we could become something other than what we were each created to be—an innocent, unbounded, omnipotent Spirit of Love.

Soon after my introduction to the teachings of ACIM more than 15 years ago, I recognized that the opportunities to undo my guilt were presented daily, and most often arose through my participation in relationships, notably romantic relationships and marriage. In time, I realized that the undoing of guilt or, as ACIM puts it, *the lessons of love*, continued through the experience of completing a marriage in divorce. ACIM teaches that all relationships are eternal because of the love that was extended and experienced within them and that therefore the idea of divorce being a severing of a union is an illusion that is to be corrected.

Divorce, in ACIM terms, simply means that *the form of the relationship is changing* and that, in fact, even though the physical proximity between the partners may be altered dramatically, on a mind, love, and spirit level, *no separation exists*. And it is this inseparable union that makes all encounters and all relationships "holy" opportunities, because they are the "vehicles" which, when properly understood, undo our guilt and ego-fostered self-hatred.

The undoing of the amassed unconscious guilt that we must feel whenever we are identifying ourselves as being anything other than our true self as love and innocent, abundant, omnipresent spirit, is our ultimate achievement, and the way to peace. We know that we are successful in this goal each time we forgive (undo) the ego identification and the actions which stem from that identification in another, and instead choose to be only at the effect of the other as spirit, or love. Since we can only see ourselves in another, they become our "mirror," and all that we see in them is actually a reflection of either our owned innocence, or perceived guilt. The identification we have chosen will be known by either feelings of gratitude and peace, or feelings of unrest and turmoil.

Our liberation from guilt is accomplished only when we forgive one another for making the common mistake of identity confusion, from which all suffering and pain ultimately originate. Further, all acts of fear, unkindness, anger, selfishness, scarcity, and guilt come from identifying oneself as the predominantly ego-run body.

The irreconcilable guilt imbedded within a false idea of self can only be dealt with through disowning the guilt and unknowingly projecting it onto others.

We do this projection in search of peace, yet peace can never be achieved in a way that is incongruent with love's laws. We are subject to the laws by which we were created, and the fundamental law of love is based on the fact that what is given is increased. Consequently, whatever we give away must be increased in ourselves. To increase love and your awareness of innocence, you must give them away.

We have all heard the powerful saying, "The truth will set us free." And when it comes to the subject of true forgiveness, the truth is we are only at the effects of love, since that is what we are. We are eternal love, eternally innocent, and endlessly unbounded, while being unified in all that is love, authentic, and true. In light of this truth, I invite you to filter all further questions, choices, and decisions through the lens of forgiveness.

Today belongs to love. Let me not fear.

A Course in Miracles

# Introduction

I believe that each of us has a journey that is meant to reveal our inner strength and, through some form of alchemy, to turn what is within us "from brass into gold." Every relationship we enter into has at its core the goal of teaching us something about ourselves that we could not have learned otherwise. The person we choose to be in a relationship with is a very specific and crucial learning partner whom we have unconsciously "contracted" into our life's journey. Spouses or partners in a committed relationship have the capacity to bring us to our knees, and in so doing, to awaken within us dormant yet powerful forces that we are destined to discover and, through grace, apply in shaping our future.

The process of separation and divorce is heart-wrenching, to say the least. It will expose much that is deeply hidden within our minds as it reveals unexplored fears and beliefs that have been binding us, often without our knowledge. Divorce exposes and mercilessly drags forth our buried and long forgotten emotional hurts. The process, although sobering, has a powerfully transformative capacity that invites us to reevaluate everything in our lives. Divorce causes us to stand face to face with our deepest fears and then transcend them. Divorce requires us to make hard choices, and it calls to us to take personal responsibility for the many decisions that greet us and will sculpt our futures. Ultimately, the process of divorce will magnify not only our light and strength, but also our most shadowed qualities and characteristics, so that we might explore ourselves more honestly. The unveiling of what we have denied or avoided, but which must be dealt with now, can indeed feel unnerving—for some even terrifying. This is natural. However, the divorce process is designed to invite us to find and reclaim our power in spite of our fears!

When we are afraid to make a decision, it is often because we do not feel as though we have enough information to choose the wisest outcome. Therefore, creating partnerships and alliances and hiring highly skilled people to educate and guide you in your decision-making is a critical first step. Undoubtedly, the pull to just stick your head in the sand and hand over your key decisions to someone you hope (or pray) is more educated or experienced than you to make your decisions is very appealing, but *it is not empowering*! Empowerment and divorce are two words that you want to unite, and you want to strive towards empowerment with every decision you make. Commit to uniting only with those individuals who are dedicated to empowering both you and your former spouse equally in the choices that will arise. Together, you and your spouse can make the decisions *that the two of you will ultimately have to live with*.

Also, divorce acts as a pendulum swinging between what has been our primary focus and what will drive us in the future. It reveals many things about the way we deal with both life and death within our lives. The way we approach our beginnings and endings is an immeasurably important thing to learn about ourselves. Whether or not we compete in a relationship will unveil our true emotional rather than chronological age. And miraculously, if we are truthful and face just how "old" we really are and work to "grow up," the process will mature us into emotional adulthood. Divorce reveals our *current* sense of self as it illuminates our fractures and whether or not we are strong enough to ensure that our actions will include the betterment of those whom we love—and once loved.

And inasmuch as divorce is a death, it is also a rebirth. It is the simultaneous surrendering of a once cherished dream unrealized, and the seeding of a new and exciting life. Understandably, we will undergo a breadth of deep feelings, including fear, guilt, sadness, rage, anger, littleness, pain, hurt, sorrow, and emptiness. We will also at times feel love, strength, hope, happiness, warmth, inspiration, contentment, and gratitude. The ocean of feelings with its rolling waves that rise and fall can, on any given day, cause us to feel crazy!

I know this to be true because I've lived it—with three different men, on three separate occasions, over a 24-year time span. I have experienced divorce in very different ways, ranging from brutal to compassionate. My first divorce was ugly and cruel, and it is shared in this book. My second divorce was uneventful because I had gone numb long before the marriage ended. That marriage had died years before the divorce came to pass. My third experience of a separation was short-lived, yet powerfully transformative—and it was with my current husband.

My first marriage, which I entered into when I was just 17 and seven months pregnant—with another man's child—lasted four years. Together, my husband in that marriage, then aged 19, and I produced two daughters. We were parents to three girls under the age of four and, still being children ourselves, were ill equipped in many ways to do the difficult work that is required of the partners in a marriage.

The marriage was brutally painful, as it was laced with infidelity and psychological and emotional cruelty. My husband had never really wanted to marry me in the first place. Consequently, the same pain that thrived within the marriage visited us in our divorce. The divorce process and the custody battle took over three years to complete. And to this day, the emotional scars resulting from the court decision to give him the primary care of the girls remain on all my children, particularly my still alienated daughter. After 21 years, she remains largely absent from her siblings' life and from mine.

It was this divorce experience that caused me to become so passionate about working with, and facilitating healing between, separating and divorcing couples. It was this heart-wrenching divorce that has made me an expert on the impacts of custody fights and, in particular, Parent Alienation Syndrome and its lifelong effects.

My daughters, two of whom were under the "spell" of Parent Alienation Syndrome for 14 years, as well as the daughter who still is under that spell, are deeply scarred. The impact of this syndrome will forever shape their futures and the way they would handle a divorce and any future custody decisions that may result from their ending any parenthood relationships they might enter into. Children who have been influenced by Parent Alienation Syndrome are also difficult to integrate into new marital unions.

Parent Alienation Syndrome is a label given when children have been prevented, emotionally, psychologically, and geographically, from having a loving relationship with one of their parents. One of the parents is making the children feel guilty for loving the other parent. Some children are punished psychologically for wanting a relationship with the alienated parent. This was what my daughter endured. Normally when this occurs, one of the parties of the divorcing couple is using the child or the children to hurt or manipulate the other parent for unresolved pain they are harboring. In my case, it was the new woman in my first husband's life who was the instigator of this syndrome.

Although some parents feel justified in sheltering or alienating the child, or removing the child's other parent from their life, this is often done under the mask of some perceived or imagined abuse that the noncustodial parent is being accused of and thus punished for. All this is accomplished under the pretext that the parent is protecting the child from the abuser. All cases of Parent Alienation Syndrome emerge as a result of deep hatred that is felt by the custodial parent towards their former spouse. If abuse were, in fact, happening, the abusive parent should still be permitted to have a relationship with their child; the relationship would just need to be supervised to protect the child. Once unrecognized by the courts, Parent Alienation Syndrome is now widely acknowledged for its long-ranging impact on the relationship between a parent and their child or children.

My second marriage produced two sons, and this union was also rocky, due to our unhealed pasts, the custody battle that lived within our courtship, and the emotional baggage we both brought into the marital merger. Gambling and alcohol abuse were the final crippling factors that contributed to the completion of the marriage.

My third experience of "divorce" was following a common-law relationship with my current husband of twelve years. Then a confirmed bachelor, he was ill prepared to deal with me, a woman with five children from three previous relationships. We separated for two months, and I agreed to an *unfair* settlement of our "blended assets" following an 18-month-period of living together. My agreement to leave with whatever Allan deemed to be fair was done without counsel of any kind. In retrospect, I believe that this was due to my optimistic nature, my emotional immaturity, and my head's being stuck in the clouds of fantasy instead of on the planet of reason. Naïvely, I just supposed everything would work out *somehow*. Looking back, I suspect that if we had not reconciled, I may well have needed to return to Allan with a request for a *fair* settlement.

The initial stages of our developing relationship involved the difficult work of blending families and the sudden and abrupt moving in and out of my then 13-year-old daughter. The ongoing issues of securing some visitation rights to my estranged girls deeply tainted our common-law union and eventually contributed to its end. We recommitted to one another two months after our "divorce" and became wedded a year later.

From each of these divorce experiences, I grew and learned things about myself that I was not so proud of. I also discovered that I had an incredible capacity to love and forgive my former husbands, my current husband, Allan, and even myself. In fact, the most remarkable growth for me came through my learning to love, understand, and appreciate my first husband's second wife—the woman with whom he had had an affair while we were still married and I was pregnant with his daughter!

In this book, I will share parts of my personal story, in hopes of awakening you to the awareness of the stormy waters we tread when the ego, rather than our mature self, navigates us while we are swimming through the emotional "ocean" that the completion of a marriage is. I will also share some crucial steps to take along the way to not only survive, but to actually heal and grow into a stronger and wiser you. Lastly, I will provide you with some tools, principles, and ideas to aid in the crucial healing that is necessary for all who are touched by a divorce. You will also have the opportunity to work with *The New Divorce Paradigm Journal*, which accompanies this book.

# The 12 Integrity Divorce Principles™

1) You are the decision maker in your life. You decide whether an event is evaluated as positive or negative. It is our values and desires that shape our judgments and evaluations.

2) People are not really committed to people; they are committed to themselves. They are committed to what they need to feel safe, view as missing from their life, or feel they are in danger of losing. People are committed to their values, models, and ideals.

3) All events are perfectly balanced. A "happy" event will always be paired with an "unhappy" one; this is inescapable. In fact, we will see that all events have both a positive and a negative "spin" (effect) to them, if we are willing to look.

4) Energy cannot be created or destroyed; it can only be transformed. Therefore, there is nothing missing; there is just a *new form* of whatever we need to manifest in our new life and our destiny.

5) Anything and anyone you do not love and appreciate as they are, you will eventually *create, attract,* or *become,* until you do love and appreciate them. This is the CAB Principle©.

6) You always attract yourself to yourself; you do this so you can own and appreciate all your hidden, unrecognized, and unloved traits. We call this mirroring.

7) The only thing that is ever lacking from any situation is that which you are unwilling to give to that situation. Most often, this is compassion and pardon.

8) Whatever you give, you will eventually receive.

9) Our need to be right is driven by our immature ego, while our mature spirit prefers being happy over being right.

10) Your thoughts become your experience, so that you can awaken to the power of your beliefs— both the known and the unrecognized ones.

11) Growth, wisdom, and strength come from a blending of support and challenge. Welcome both.

12) Apologies heal.

On the following pages, we will explore how these principles can be applied and integrated into the divorce process.

# Integrating the 12 Integrity Divorce Principles™

## INTEGRITY DIVORCE PRINCIPLE NO. 1

*You are the decision maker in your life.*
*You decide whether an event*
*is evaluated as positive or negative.*
*It is our values and desires that shape*
*our judgments and evaluations.*

Each of us has adopted ideas and ideals of how to live and how to be and has woven together a set of behaviors which in our minds define the "ideal" of a role, such as mother, father, friend, sibling, co-worker, and so on. In addition, we have within us "pictures" of what actions and events are deemed to be either good or bad, and unconsciously we measure all events against those inner "ideal images." For instance, an image of a flower garden is by many evaluated as "better" than a garden full of scrap metal. If, however, you are a mechanic or a welder, your view may well be opposite to that of those who prefer flowers to steel! So, who is "right"?

Unfortunately, what we have not been conditioned to ask ourselves often enough is, "Is my value or ideal really better than someone else's?" In truth, it is not. Each of our internalized ideals and presumed "good pictures," which make us feel safe, comfortable, in power, and good, is there to do that, and nothing more. We grow as people through having a blending of both support and challenge, so we ultimately need both gardens!

Each of us can dramatically soften the experience of divorce by choosing to evaluate each individual's internal ideals as valuable, and by reclaiming our right to say that all events are really neither "bad" nor "good"—they are simply necessary opportunities for growth!

## INTEGRITY DIVORCE PRINCIPLE NO. 2

---

*People are not really committed to people; they are committed to themselves.*
*They are committed to what they need to feel safe, view as missing from their life, or feel they are in danger of losing.*
*People are committed to their values, models, and ideals.*

---

Most of humanity is afraid. Many people hold an internalized belief that they are lacking something. This belief is terrifying, and we desperately want not to be afraid and inferior to others. We believe we are not smart enough, rich enough, nice enough, forgiving enough, tough enough, caring enough, and the list is unending! For this reason, we become obsessed and unconsciously driven to attain our perceived lacks and voids—sometimes at the risk of neglecting or hurting the people we love. The sobering truth is: we are often committed to feeling powerful and unafraid, more than being committed to another person. However, if we are with someone whose presence causes feelings of power and self-acceptance to arise within us, we will feel attracted to, and maybe even fall in love with, that individual!

Even our internalized "ideal role models" unconsciously run us! The attainment of being a "perfect parent," for instance, has caused both joy and sorrow for those pursuing that goal and the surrounding family members. An individual who strives to be "perfect" does so because they believe they will be "better than," safer, more powerful, and more loved and appreciated if they succeed.

Since perfection is really only possible when it is equated with a definition of love, each parent who loves is ultimately already perfect! Those who believe specific actions and behaviors can create a model of a perfect parent will undoubtedly never really accomplish the goal, since we all hold differing beliefs about what is evaluated as a model of good and perfect behavior.

## INTEGRITY DIVORCE PRINCIPLE NO. 3

*All events are perfectly balanced. A "happy" event will always be paired with an "unhappy" one; this is inescapable. In fact, we will see that all events have both a positive and a negative "spin" (effect) to them, if we are willing to look.*

The world we live in is dualistic in nature. All things are known by their opposite. Happy is inseparable from unhappy. This is so because consciousness itself is a mind function, and the mind is actually in a constant state of equilibrium or balance, even though we are often unaware of this fact.

In reality, our unawareness of the constant equilibrium that supports us and all experience is what causes us to experience suffering. For instance, winning a lottery ticket, for most of us, will at first seem to be only "good," but upon a deeper evaluation, it will be revealed that greed, selfishness, untrustworthiness, confinement, secrecy, obligation, and irresponsibility will also be the companions of the initial "good" component of such a windfall!

A part of the mind is addicted to the attainment of pleasure without pain, and so it blinds our perception of the opposite. This "blindness" causes emotional highs followed by emotional lows, in an unending rollercoaster.

If we wise up and look, we will indeed see that all events bring with them equal proportions of the opposite "agent" determined by us and equal proportions of however "high" or "low" we have become by the evaluation of the event. So, if winning a lottery ticket registered as a 10 for a high, one would look for a 10 in the low. The lows can be culminated from either one aspect, greed, evaluated as 10, or from several aspects added together, for instance selfishness (2), untrustworthiness (1), confinement (2), secrecy (1), obligation(1), and irresponsibility(3) to recognize the equality of both the positive and negative sides.

We can remain stable and calm, rather than manic, simply by seeking for the "hidden" opposites that are always present.

## INTEGRITY DIVORCE PRINCIPLE NO. 4

*Energy cannot be created or destroyed; it can only be transformed. Therefore, there is nothing missing; there is just a new form of whatever we need to manifest in our new life and our destiny.*

If we look honestly back upon our lives, we will notice that whatever or whomever we needed did show up for us in some form when we felt it or they were missing. For instance, my mother left my life when I was 19, so if I needed a "mother," someone else who embodied the traits and qualities of what it means to be "maternal" miraculously came into my life to fulfill my desire. When I review the whole of my life, I can find a chain of individuals, male and female, young and old, who all played the role of "mother" to ensure that whenever I needed a "mom," *I had one.*

Since the surrogate mom was not my real mother and sometimes not even a woman, they will have "magically" provided the care, concern, protection, guidance, nurturance, and so on, that I was yearning for. This person will unknowingly have filled the role of mother whenever I felt that my mom was missing.

If we are blinded to the awareness that every need we have is actually simultaneously met in the moment our desire arises to have something, we feel as though there are things, people, financial freedom, and other aspects that are missing. This is an illusion. There is, in fact, never ever anything missing! What we need to achieve any dream or goal is actually around us in an unrecognized form. It is present in different forms, often in forms in which we are less accustomed to having the item of our desire, such as was shown in the mother analogy above.

Energy, which can be both material (a body) and nonmaterial (an idea) in form, is in a constant dance of change, moving from form to form, materialized and dematerialized, as it is necessary to support the human experience.

Even if you believe you do not have enough money, for instance, this is an idea, based upon a presumption that money comes only in certain "forms," such as coins, bills, checks, and drafts. Money is actually a globally agreed-upon form of trade which is used to create fair exchange. But you can also create fair exchange by trading time, expertise, knowledge, ideas, information, physical effort, an asset, precious metal, stones, or minerals. So, considering this model of money, we all have it!

The trick to finding one's real wealth comes in finding it in all its forms, and evaluating them. What are your limbs worth? What is your sanity worth? What is your health worth? Most of us would say these are priceless, which means we have assets that invalidate any thought of being impoverished, or even broke.

*Anything and anyone you do not love and appreciate as they are, you will eventually create, attract, or become, until you do love and appreciate them. This is the CAB Principle©.*

We are destined to love, which involves the complete transcendence of the idea of judgment. Our judgments are always based upon adopted individual ideals and values, and so they eventually must be surrendered as justification to judge at all.

The self-empowering reality is that we can only see in another some aspect of ourselves which we either appreciate or disown. This is a fact, so if we judge, which means we cut off a part of ourselves, we will have to attract it back towards us in order to love it. To love something, you need to know it fully, and see and appreciate both sides of it. Ultimately, through understanding something or someone fully, we can come to appreciate and love it or them as they are.

If we refuse to do so, we will attract, through a myriad of people and experiences, that which we feel is unlovable until we believe otherwise. For many of us, it would take many lifetimes to achieve such a goal.

INTEGRITY DIVORCE PRINCIPLE NO. 6

*You always attract yourself to yourself; you do this so you can own and appreciate all your hidden, unrecognized, and unloved traits. We call this mirroring.*

How others treat us is a direct reflection of how we treat ourselves! Most of us have an internal dialogue which is much harsher than any dialogue that any other person would have with us. This is so because over the years, we have gathered up all the misunderstandings we have encountered and the unkind words that resulted from them and have systematically bundled them together to use as justification for our self-defiling punishment.

If you want to change the ways others treat you, you must begin by examining your inner beliefs about yourself, your self-worth, and being deserving of great joy and love. When you truly believe that you are a valuable and wealthy member of humanity, others will begin to treat you as such to "mirror" those beliefs. Your inner beliefs direct all outward experience, so think magnificent thoughts!

## INTEGRITY DIVORCE PRINCIPLE NO. 7

> *The only thing that is ever lacking from any situation is that which you are unwilling to give to that situation. Most often, this is compassion and pardon.*

A trap that many of us fall into is playing the victim. Instead, let's strive to be the victor, and let's begin by asking ourselves what is necessary for us to do, in this situation, to foster the most beneficial outcome for all involved, instead of defaulting to blame.

Remember that, in essence, we are all innocent, radiant, and loving beings, and in any moment that we forget this identification for either our former spouse, our child(ren), or ourselves, we become afraid and often unkind. To correct this misidentification, compassion and pardon are needed to return to our authentic "self" and a more mutually supportive outcome.

## Whatever you give, you will eventually receive.

Many of us have heard the old familiar phrase that *life is a cul-de-sac, and what goes in, must eventually come out!* And while I believe that all actions offered to others are ultimately offered to us, I also believe that this is true because we are learning, collectively as humans, to give only love, if we want to have only love.

Because giving and receiving are one and the same, we must think carefully about what we give. I like to live my life as if there were someone always watching my every move. I like to believe that the most valuable things are those which are increased by sharing them—things like love, kindness, caring, ideas, and compliments. I have found that if I consider this Integrity principle before I act, I am far less likely to give away unkindness, selfishness, or greed.

*Our need to be right is driven by our immature ego, while our mature spirit prefers being happy over being right.*

This Integrity principle is a direct assault upon the ego identification that we at times envelop! The ego much prefers to be right over having peace, since it is itself the adopted idea of being a wounded, inferior, and isolated self. The insecurities that inevitably arise from such an identification spawn the desire to compete and be in constant defense.

The ego vacillates between suspiciousness and viciousness, depending upon how afraid and insecure it is feeling in any situation. Spirit, on the other hand, is in need of nothing.

When we feel safe, we are kinder and gentler than when we feel threatened. If either we or our values and goals are perceived to be threatened, we jump into a defensive stance. *Choosing* to allow others to be right, instead of you and your opinions, defines your emotional and psychological maturity, and it welcomes peace instead of war.

The need to be right, rather than wrong, comes from a deeply seated fear that if we were wrong, we would be less lovable, less intelligent, and more vulnerable than others, and thus exposed to embarrassment.

Coming to terms with the reality that we will all at times be mistaken, less likeable, less intelligent, more vulnerable, and embarrassed, and *we will survive it all,* will liberate us greatly.

## INTEGRITY DIVORCE PRINCIPLE No. 10

*Your thoughts become your experience, so that you can awaken to the power of your beliefs—both the known and the unrecognized ones.*

Have you ever really stopped to evaluate which beliefs you hold that may not be true? The ideas and beliefs we have adopted are often unknowingly running our lives more than we are. To co-create a life in which we are the star and the lead actor means that we must examine the thoughts that we hold, to determine whether they are truthful or illusory. One example of an illusory thought would be the globally accepted idea that divorce is bad. Divorce is neither bad nor good—it is simply a word defining the experience of completing a contract between two people. Another common belief is that you can't meet a future life partner in bars, yet that is where I met my current husband! (I never did subscribe to that belief.) Another frequently held belief is that being old equates to being less attractive, or completely unattractive.

If we repeatedly experienced being lied to, we would be wise to question if we are able to hear the truth and remain calm and receptive regardless of what the other person tells us. If we are unwilling to hear the truth when it is painful, then we will unconsciously attract dishonesty.

If we repeatedly find ourselves being taken advantage of, we could explore a possible inner belief that we are more lovable if we are a martyr or doormat! Neither is really true; it is only true for the believer of that thought! *As a person thinketh, so they are!*

Ultimately, our beliefs become our experience regardless of their validity or truthfulness, so as you transition from married to single life, take time each day to explore what beliefs need to be deleted from the hard drive of your mind and which ones you would like to inscribe there instead.

INTEGRITY DIVORCE PRINCIPLE NO. 11

## Growth, wisdom, and strength come from a blending of support and challenge. Welcome both.

When we are green, we are growing, and when we are ripe, we rot! If ever we are under the belief we have no more to learn or to offer to the world, we can be assured that we are preparing to leave the physical experience.

Perhaps if we look back upon the more difficult experiences that we have survived, we will also discover that we experienced tremendous growth in strength, endurance, and wisdom at that time as well. This is true because we grow from a blending of support and challenge, and so that is what is magnetically drawn into our lives each moment. Too much support fosters laziness and codependence; not enough support causes withdrawal, anger, and depression. The truth is that we always have equal servings of both, but we are often under the spell of the addictive part of the mind, which seeks the highs and lows made by denying the other half.

Next time either a supportive or challenging event occurs, look for the drawback of the supportive event and the benefits of the challenging one to stay aware of the perfect equilibrium of your life!

## *Apologies heal.*

There is an undeniable power to heal in the wake of the words, "I am truly sorry." Our ego evaporates into nothingness when we find the courage to say that we are sorry for a behavior or action that caused another person pain.

In the many years of marriage and divorce counseling and coaching that I have done, I have not found a more powerfully transformative set of words that one person can say to another. The words seem to help a wounded individual to separate the person from the behavior which caused them to suffer. Further, these sweet words can rebuild trust because in being offered them, the offended party feels recognized and understood. Apologies heal because they restore hope while building a bridge of new beginnings. Sincere apologies bridge the past to the present and set free a new and untarnished future.

## Journal Exercise:

Beginning on page 23 in your *New Divorce Paradigm Journal*, please write down how each principle might impact the divorce process.

## Chapter One

# My Journey: What We Do for Love

INTEGRITY DIVORCE PRINCIPLE NO. 1

*You are the decision maker in your life.*
*You decide whether an event*
*is evaluated as positive or negative.*
*It is our values and desires that shape*
*our judgments and evaluations.*

It was December 1984. My newborn daughter Sara was barely three weeks old, and I needed some support in dealing with the reality that Adam, my husband of four years, was going to leave me for another woman, Eve. "From here on in, it will just be the three girls and I," I thought. Clearly, I was heartbroken. I drove from our home in Lethbridge to Calgary to stay with a friend and figure out how I would manage life on my own with three young children. During the evening of my arrival there, Sara became very, very ill. I took her to Calgary Children's Hospital, where she was admitted immediately. It was discovered that she had bronchial pneumonia, and her life was in danger. They shaved her tiny head, hooked her up to an IV, and eventually to life support. The doctors weren't sure if she would survive. They advised me to inform her father in case she would not live until the morning. Now Sara and I were both fighting to survive—she physically and I emotionally.

I called Adam at the restaurant where he worked. He answered the phone, and I informed him of the seriousness of the situation. I told him that he should come to Calgary to see Sara. He reluctantly agreed, but said I would have to come and pick him up, since he had no vehicle that could make the trip. I agreed.

It's a two-hour drive between Calgary and Lethbridge; I made it in 90 minutes. It was 11:30 P.M. when I arrived at the hotel. I walked into the dining room to meet Adam. He announced that he had decided not to come with me after all. I was shocked and confused; I pleaded, he refused, and I left.

I went across the street to the gas station and called my friend in Calgary to check on my two girls, whom she was watching. I needed to let her know what had happened; I was crying and trying to sort out my thoughts and the appropriate actions. I told her that on my way back, I would swing by my house and get some extra clothes for the girls, since I would undoubtedly be in Calgary much longer than I had originally anticipated. I told her I would stop by her house to leave the extra clothes and then head back to the hospital. I finished the conversation stating that I did not know how long I would be at the hospital, but that I would keep her informed.

Approximately 20 minutes later, I pulled up to my home to discover Eve's car parked in front of my house. I felt confused and shattered as I searched for a reason other than what was obvious, why she would be at our home. Apparently, Adam still had a key, and since Eve had a roommate, her place did not offer them the privacy they wanted, so they had come here, thinking that I wouldn't be home.

I walked into the house; Adam and Eve were both inside, startled by my sudden entry into the living room. I was speechless as I saw a blanket, a bottle of wine, some movies, crackers, and cheese all neatly laid out on my living room floor. They were preparing for a romantic picnic... I lost my composure and began crying, raging, and pleading for some understanding. Then, suddenly, instinctual childlike and maternal feelings flooded my body. I was like a mother bear that perceived her cubs to be in danger. I ran up the stairs to the kitchen, began scanning the drawers, and grabbed the largest knife I could find. I had never felt such rage; I felt disorientated, and my heart ached in disbelief. I felt completely abandoned, emotionally and physically — time stood still.

Suddenly, a wave of warmth filled my being and an inner voice said, "Put down the knife. The baby needs you, the girls need you, and this is not the answer." Defeated, I surrendered. I listened to the voice and set down the knife. I left the house and got in my car. I cried and told Jesus that this was too much to bear. I begged for help as I sobbed, barely able to see the road through my tears.

To this day, I have no memory of the trip that followed. The only memory I have is of the moment I suddenly found myself at a stoplight at the Southland Drive intersection on the edge of Calgary. It felt like only a moment had passed from the time I raced down the highway to get back to the hospital, to the time I sat waiting for the light to turn green. Within moments, I was rounding the corner to my girlfriend's house. I knocked softly, then again; the porch light came on, and she cracked the door open. Speechless she stood, staring at me, "How did you get here so fast?" she asked. "I drove," I replied. "That can't be—you called me about 25 minutes ago." I was too confused to get her point. All I wanted to do was to get to my baby girl before she died. I dropped off the clothing and headed downtown to see if Sara was still alive. When I arrived at the hospital, she was still in critical condition; she remained in this state for three days, after which a miraculous turnaround began.

Weeks passed, and Sara fully recovered. With her recovery came the torture of fully accepting the idea that I was going to be on my own with three little children. Although Adam and I had separated before, we had always come back together shortly after the birth of each of the first two babies. This time, I just knew things were going to be different. I was consumed by my racing mind, desperately trying to figure out a way to get Adam back. I deeply wanted our family to be back together and, in spite of all the problems and perceived abuse, I wanted to be his wife.

Adam was confused also, so he was alternately telling both Eve and me that he wanted to be with us, and was "arranging" it. For the next three weeks, he would flip-flop between beds, and then I had finally had enough. I arranged for a babysitter and drove to Eve's house, where they were living together. It was about 1 P.M. I knocked, she answered; she seemed without surprise, and wanted to talk with me.

We decided to go to the Boston Pizza down the street, where we talked for six hours. We talked about everything from my childhood to their great sex life. My motive for the talk was to see what was so "special" about her—to identify it and, if at all possible, duplicate it, so I could get Adam back. After spending some time with her, I realized that she would probably have become a friend had we met under different circumstances. She was warm, sincere, and pretty. In fact, I saw a lot of personality similarities between us, and I could see why Adam had fallen for her.

In spite of everything, however, I still wanted to understand why she was willing to tear apart our family. I wanted to understand why she would date a married man who was expecting a new baby. In response, she said that Adam had initially told her that his marriage was over and that there was no chance of reconciliation, and that she had believed him.

She shared with me her childhood and how her mother had died when she was 13. She told me that she had been hospitalized for psychiatric assessment in the months to follow because of her depressed and uncontrollable behavior. In addition, she shared how hard her childhood had been. She had suffered greatly because of her alcoholic father. At a young age, she had become involved in an incestuous relationship. It became obvious to me that she was troubled by her past, just as Adam and I were troubled by our respective pasts.

I wanted to let Eve know that Adam had been telling me that he couldn't get rid of her because she wouldn't let go of him—that he really loved me, and that he wanted our family back. She was stunned by my messages, because Adam was telling her exactly the same things about me. In my heart, I knew that she was telling the truth and that a very confused puppeteer was playing her and me like puppets. I told her then that I was through with Adam, and that she could have him.

Even though I had made my decision, I wanted to know why she felt that she loved him so much. This turned out to have been the wrong question to ask! Eve told me, with a glow of certainty, that Adam was "the guy"—the soulmate that she had been looking for, and she had never been so happy. She was amazed by how loving and caring Adam was—not only to her, but to his girls also. She told me how he cared for her, ironed her work clothes, tidied the house, and rubbed her back. I was stunned. He had never washed a dish in our home, not even when I had delivered our babies.

Eve then dropped the final bomb on my heart by innocently mentioning that she had watched the two older girls while I was delivering Sara. How could he, I thought. He had *her* watch my girls, while I delivered our baby—how sick! "He never rubbed *my* back, ironed *my* clothes, or did any of the other things you say he does for you," I told Eve. I was confused. Were we talking about the same person?

After our discussion, we drove to Adam's place of work, where we both announced that we were done with him. I went home. A few hours later, he called me on the phone, sobbing and pleading with me to talk to Eve and convince her that he and I were, in fact, finished. He said he was certain that she was his soulmate and that he was sorry for all the pain and suffering he had put me through. He admitted that he had never felt for me what he was feeling for her. He assured me that he really loved her and couldn't bear to live without her. He pleaded with me to help save their relationship, since we were through. I thought about it, realized that my relationship with him was over, and agreed to call Eve. I called her and assured her that since he had done so much for her, he must deeply care for her. I reminded her that if he was her soulmate, she should not just cast him away. She listened; I assured her that I no longer wanted to be his wife, and they made up.

## Chapter Two

# Choices

Integrity Divorce Principle No. 2

*People are not really committed to people;*
*they are committed to themselves.*
*They are committed to what they need to feel*
*safe, view as missing from their life,*
*or feel they are in danger of losing.*
*People are committed to their values,*
*models, and ideals.*

## You, the Student and Decision Maker

Each of us is a student and must make decisions to grow and learn of our power and resilience. Each of us is also entertained and spoken to by two very different internal guides. One guide is altruistic in nature, representing the voice of wisdom and fairness, while the other is self-absorbed, afraid, and defensive. To picture it, I invite you to remember watching the Saturday morning cartoons. Remember Sylvester the cat and Tweety Bird? On one Saturday morning, when I was watching the survival "dance" between Tweety and Sylvester, I learned some very powerful things that stuck with me. The first was that goodness and truth would always eventually prevail. And the second was that we are decision makers and that who or what we listen to affects our experiences.

Sylvester had Tweety in his paws and was about to swallow him, when suddenly two characters arrived—one on each of Sylvester's shoulders. An angel kitty sat on his right shoulder, and on the other shoulder was the devilish cat. Each called forth a part of Sylvester's nature—the shadow or the light, and each wanted to see its side win. In this case, the student and decision maker was Sylvester. And as so many times before, he chose the devilish cat over the angel kitty! But...since good always prevails in the end, in the final hour or, in this case, millisecond, the angel kitty rescued Tweety just before Sylvester swallowed him.

When moving through a divorce, we may well feel at times like we want to listen to the devilish cat, too, and swallow and destroy our mate! However, there is another way, and each of us is a decision maker who can choose the way to take.

We can follow one of two very different guides; both are counting on us to follow their thoughts and beliefs.

So, step one in moving through the divorce process is the recognition that we are the decision maker, *the Student*, who can often forget that we must choose between two internal guides who live within our minds.

Since each guide is very different from the other, and each is promoting a different thought system, our choice is critically important. Each guide embodies an archetype. An archetype is the culmination of a collection of traits, characteristics, and qualities which, when bundled together, become a single entity representing those qualities. For example, if I say, "She is such a mother," you will immediately think of a host of qualities and traits which represent the embodiment of "mother." Traits and qualities such as warm, nurturing, caring, protective, and provider will come to mind. Bundle them all up, and you have the archetype of "Mother."

In our minds, we have two guides, who also embody two archetypes. The *Teacher* and the *Warrior* each have their own agenda, but they are diametrically opposed.

The *Teacher* promotes a thought system which is based upon love in that it fosters care, kindness, compassion, and generosity. In opposition is the *Warrior* whose thought system is based on fear, which ignites feelings of lack, loss, anger, revenge, and attack. The *Teacher* is the voice that stands for fairness and equality. Its thought system is based on truth, unification, love, and wisdom. The other guide, the *Warrior*, is the voice of division, separation, and inequality, and its thought system is based on fear, lack, guilt, judgment, and autonomy.

The *Warrior* believes that you are in danger, and thus fear is the fuel that keeps it alive. It directs that you need to defend and protect, to look out for number one—you! At all costs, it instructs that guilt is mandatory, and so it is content *only* when either you or your spouse is guilty. Another crippling fact about the *Warrior* is that it is just as happy to allow you both to be guilty. So, provided you fluctuate between either of you being the guilty one, the ego's insatiable hunger is curbed, but never satisfied. Guilt and fear are the source and need of this warrior, who therefore is in constant pursuit of both.

Both fear and guilt are fueled by the belief that you or someone else has done or will do something that caused or will cause more pain than pleasure, or more challenge than support. Fear, which is always future-based, and guilt, which is always about the past, are what keeps us out of the present moment, where we can think most clearly. Many people are under the belief that there can be a situation or event that is out of equilibrium. This belief is an illusion, as will be discussed later in this chapter.

Respectively, the *Warrior* and the *Teacher* within our minds show us about our capacity to choose either the "high road" paved with love and wisdom, or the "low road" gleaming with treasures of victimhood, guilt, and shame. The "high road" is a path of integrity and fairness that leads home to your authentic self. It takes you towards choices that heal instead of wound, holding dear the present moment for purposes of transcending the past. On the contrary, the "low road," which is *Warrior*-occupied, leads to decisions furthering fear, judgment, self-righteousness, and autonomy. Each path does indeed have a goal and purpose, but they are diametrically opposed. You as the *Student* must decide upon a path—either the "high road" of authentic power and integrity, or the "low road," which does indeed elicit force—the hungry path of brutality.

Consider that the hardest decisions we make—those based upon taking the "high road"—won't be made for us alone. They will be made for the betterment of our new life, our family, our future, and, most importantly, our children.

Remember Integrity Divorce Principle No. 7, which says that *the only thing that is ever lacking from any situation is that which you are unwilling to give to that situation. Most often, this is compassion and pardon.*

## My Journey: A Mother's Love

It was five months after the birth of Sara, my third daughter. Following an enormous struggle to regain some of my self-esteem, lost because of the infidelity in our marriage, Adam, my first husband, made a suggestion that forever changed the direction in which our lives went. He suggested that he and his girlfriend, Eve, would take the girls to live with them. Initially I was outraged, and I refused. A week later, the same request came again, as he told me that if I really loved the girls, I would do what was best for them, not me. That comment hit me right in the gut. My withered sense of self due to my tumultuous childhood and Adam's repeated infidelity had so crippled me that I began to entertain the idea. It was true that I was struggling in every area in my life— emotionally, psychologically, and financially. I was working long hours at multiple jobs and could no longer find the resources to give more than I was giving, but he could, and he reminded me of that weekly. My heart and head felt torn apart, moving me in opposing directions. The whole idea of moving the children into his care reminded me of a childhood story I had heard in Sunday School of King Solomon and the two mothers. As I recalled the biblical story, King Solomon was asked to decide on who was the true mother, since they both claimed the child as their own. His decision to divide the baby in half whirled through my mind. What would love have me do?

In the biblical story, there is a dispute over the baby between the natural mother and the acting mother. Both claim to be the real mother wanting to keep the child. The opposing parties are both proclaiming a deep and unconditional love for the child. King Solomon is not sure who is telling the truth, so he suggests that he would kill the child, offering each "mother" a half.

The acting mother seems to find this decision acceptable, while the natural mother is horrified and replies that she would rather see the child raised by the acting mother than its life taken. In some strange mythological way, it seemed that I had also been given such a choice.

The division between what my mind rationalized I should do, and what my heart and soul whispered was my ultimate journey, was tearing me apart. In my heart of hearts, I knew my soul contract was to surrender my children to "a better life than I could give them," for now.

A couple of weeks later, I surrendered my three young girls, ages three and two, and six months. I wanted desperately to believe that, if the three of us adults worked together to co-parent, it would be better for the children than what I alone could ever do for them. But while it could have been a beautiful way to co-parent the girls, this was not what Adam and Eve had secretly planned. Initially, I agreed to a trial period of this new arrangement and moved the girls from my place to Adam and Eve's house for the summer. Packing up my daughters' rooms was one of the hardest things I have ever done.

This event reminded me of a movie I had seen just months before, of a Jewish mother leaving for the concentration camps. Merrill Streep acted as a Jewish mother who was being sent away. In one scene, she was asked to choose between her daughter and her son. The soldier indicated that, through her choice, one would be freed, while the other would go with her to die. That's how I felt; death was now a lever of life, and that day, a part of me died.

The weeks following were excruciatingly painful for me. I would go and visit the children between jobs and then, as I was preparing to leave for work, the girls would cry, begging me not to leave them as they clung to my leg. Each time I had to leave them, another piece of my heart was torn out, guilt consumed me, and in time I began to go numb. Soon I began avoiding the visits, believing they were too hard on the girls. I didn't realize, however, that Eve was feeling abandoned by me, and in time I would understand the huge impact that Eve's perception of her abandonment by me would have on the next 14 years of my life. By the end of August, I couldn't take it anymore, and thoughts of abducting the girls raced through my mind. The only thing that prevented me from doing so was that I didn't want my children to go through the same childhood experiences that I had had.

My parents divorced when I was seven; their relationship was volatile and full of rage and hate. For years, Mom hid us from my Dad. This was not a path I was prepared to have my children repeat, so for me, in my mind, there was no escape, and no answer.

I was working at three jobs to help make ends meet for myself and to help support the girls' physical needs. Eve was three months pregnant and unable to work, so I worked harder to provide for the kids and myself. Soon I stopped eating, and then sleeping; I was dying of heartbreak and was overwhelmed with guilt, remorse, and confusion regarding my actions. I could no longer reason rationally; my self-esteem evaporated, and soon, taking the girls back no longer seemed to be an option.

At midnight, in the first days of September while I was closing the bar where I worked as the assistant manager, I received a call from Eve, announcing that she, Adam, and the girls would be leaving the next morning at 6 A.M. to go to Edmonton, which is six hours north of Lethbridge. "Everything has been arranged," she explained. Adam had landed a fantastic job with a great salary, they had rented a nice house, and they were going to be able to give the kids the best of everything. They were leaving in the morning, and wasn't I excited for them, she asked. She told me that I needed to give them this chance and to not stand in the way of giving the best to the girls; if I loved them, I would "not interfere."

I panicked; I was afraid I would lose them forever, so I said that I would go, too. This would buy me some time to figure things out, I thought. Maybe things would be better in Edmonton. I reasoned that I could not take this opportunity away from them if I loved them. After all, there was nothing and no one to stay in Lethbridge for. I surrendered to the idea, and at 6 A.M. the following morning, I was heading north.

## Chapter Three

# Preparing for a New Life—
# Decisions That Count

INTEGRITY DIVORCE PRINCIPLE NO. 3

*All events are perfectly balanced. A "happy" event will always be paired with an "unhappy" one; this is inescapable. In fact, we will see that all events have both a positive and a negative "spin" (effect) to them, if we are willing to look.*

The decision to complete a marriage comes with some sobering facts. The first fact is that following this decision, our lives, and those of our family members, will be forever changed. Second is the realization that we have completed a "dance" which was destined to end, or else it wouldn't have. Ultimately, all dances teach us "steps" we needed to learn. And so we will undoubtedly carry effects from the marriage dance and the relationship itself that transfer into our future. The decision to divorce will reshape us and prepare us for a different life. This is unavoidable. This realization becomes a blessing when it is owned, appreciated, and used appropriately to support our new future.

Traditionally, the decision to divorce comes with two primary fears: First is the unknown emotional impact on all involved from the changes that occur when we begin to live separate lives. Second is the uncertainty of the financial impact of dividing the couple's assets. The fear of either, and more often both, can leave us in a state of paralysis. When we are frozen with fear, we cannot use our reasoning capacities, so we make rash or fear-based decisions. The truth is that both primary issues can be guided, and both can be empowering, when we understand the laws of the physical world and its unavoidable dualistic nature.

In short, all traits and events happen in pairs. Opposites are inseparable bedfellows. Living is a lever of death, and whatever is evaluated as positive is always partnered with a negative, so up is defined by what is down, hot is paired to cold, hard joined with soft, and light is coupled to dark. When the dualism is known and appreciated and, more importantly, worked with, the divorce process is softened. The reality is that whether we stay married or proceed with divorce, there will be pleasure and pain, support and challenge, good times and sad times, too. Either way, we grow.

The success of our emotional transition is dependent on our willingness to be honest with ourselves—admitting both the shadow and light side of our persona. We all have both sides, and admitting to the shadow is easiest when we understand that the shadow is connected to the light. Therefore, kind is coupled with cruel, honest with dishonest, generous with stingy, and soft is paired with hard.

In reality, each side cancels out, or rather neutralizes, the effects of the other. The negative trait neutralizes the evaluated positive trait, leaving in its wake an equilibrated person.

This same law applies to every event. A great event will be paired with a not so great event, but we are often so infatuated with the "great one" that we are blinded and do not look for its "mate." Here is an example: One of my clients was recently told that the matrimonial home she was living in would have to be sold to pay off the debt that she and her husband had incurred. At the time that this was revealed to her, she received a call from her manager at her place of employment, advising her that she had been given the promotion and salary raise she had been seeking.

I later pointed out to my client that if she had not been wise enough to look for the gain that was accompanying the loss, she would have missed recognizing the loss/gain transformation. Seeing both events happening simultaneously keeps us aware of the laws of equilibrium.

So, rather than thinking in terms of good and bad, positive and negative, think in terms of events and qualities, and recognize that all events are opportunities to grow. And to grow into our wisest, most powerful, and caring selves, we must face ourselves—both sides. We must own both what we have judged as the shadow and the light of our natures, until we learn that both are judgments that can be transcended through acceptance. We then come to see that all events are fused with equal proportions of what we have individually selected and evaluated as being positive or negative. Once we realize that there will never be an event that does not bring with it equal proportions of positive and negative outcomes, we are free.

An important piece of this equilibrating work is to understand that we all have slightly different values and morals, desires, and needs that shape our personal evaluation of what is good or bad, positive or negative. *And we should not be so arrogant as to believe that our beliefs are right or better than those of our former spouse.*

## Values, Wants, and Desires

Had I known, or had I been instructed by my marriage counselor at the time of my first husband's affair, that he was being driven by things he wanted but which he did not perceive me as being capable or willing to give, I would have felt the impact of my first divorce very differently.

People marry to accomplish differing goals. These goals and achievements, as well as acquirements, are often driven by the partners' desires and values. For instance, Ray and Susan, who are in their late twenties, are both professors. They met two years ago, have dated seriously for the past 18 months, and are engaged to be married. They both want children soon, and they want to have summers off together to spend at Susan's and her sister's cabin.

They share the dream of wanting to raise a tight-knit family, and both feel valued and appreciated because their common primary desires weave a bond between them. Susan and Ray also enjoy outdoor sports and spend many weekends hiking. Their relationship allows them to pursue their highest values together.

Throughout their marriage, there will be a hierarchy of perceived voids, which will, in turn, drive their values, such as more children, financial freedom, a business partnership, deepened friendship, a more fiery sexual companionship, and so on. As each void becomes filled, a new desire will follow, and those desires will often be reflective of the changes that affect them as they age, mature, and evolve soulfully.

Individually and as a couple, as they move from void to void and acquire what they pursue, a new set of desires will rush in to meet them. Through continued acquisitions, they will grow in their sense of power.

Sometimes the new void that we perceive as a value and wish to attain, such as financial freedom, will require skills and drive that our current partner does not have, nor will want to acquire. When the people we are with do not wish to pursue *our primary values* with us, and especially if they are against our pursuit of these values, the relationship will begin to become strained and, in time, will likely end. When this dynamic occurs, we will begin to pursue others who value what we value at that particular stage in our life. Therefore, the reason for the next union may well be different from the one that drove the previous relationship.

In twenty years, Ray and Susan may be pursuing the achievement of golf, their own business, financial freedom, travel, or retirement. If one of them perceives that the other does not put sufficient energy into the pursuit of one or more of these primary values, then they may well be attracted to another mate who they feel is more in alignment with their values at that time.

*I wish to alert you to the hard and often shattering reality that people are really not committed to each other, unless the other person appreciates their values and desires. The hard truth is that we are really committed to ourselves. We have all set up an internal set of morals, ideal role models, desires, values, and wants which literally run our lives. We have individually created "ideal" models of parenthood, being a good spouse or partner, a good child, sibling, co-worker, team player, and friend. We covet dreams and desires of what a future painted with freedom looks like. We have an image of how much money deems us to be powerful, and what lifestyles make us feel successful and free. Many of us strive to achieve an ideal relationship, a perfect family, and the list is endless. We believe our models and ideals are "better" or "right" and will ultimately judge and evaluate others with respect to our ideals.*

In light of this, we can determine that some primary reasons for leaving a marriage may simply be that we no longer believe that our mate values what we do, and thus we feel unloved. In this dynamic, we are oblivious to the understanding that we are, in fact, more committed to meeting our needs than we are committed to our spouse. The tough truth is that we are actually in pursuit of what we feel is missing and perceive to be of great importance and, sadly, value even more than we value each other. In fact, our commitment to our mate is directly influenced by our perception of how they help us get what we desire. In fact, we married them in part because we thought they were pursuing the same dreams and desires as we. Consequently, the key to unlocking the door of future communication and negotiation is through knowing how to get each other talking, by asking questions of our spouse in the areas that are important *to them*.

What drives a desire has two components. First is an internal image of what the maximal expression of the picture would look like. Let's say the picture is complete financial freedom. The picture looks like this: $1 million in cash in the bank; all my beautiful fun and retirement properties paid for; and a nice financial portfolio that generates me a $40,000 monthly income. Now let's say I have been working towards this dream for 15 years, so in my belief, I am halfway there. The difference between where I perceive myself to be today in comparison to the "ideal" picture I hold in my mind is the driving force that keeps me going. The degree to which a part of the picture is missing is the degree to which I am committed. In this sense, then, our value is driven by our perceived void. We all look for what we think is missing, that which will make us feel powerful, free, safe, cared for, and valued. This is true in all arenas— the physical, financial, mental, emotional, spiritual, and familial. Each of us feels close to those who help us get what we want and will avoid, remove, and defend against those who hinder us in our efforts to attain our desires. Through knowing this, we begin to learn how to make each other feel valued and appreciated as we recognize the equality of the needs of both people.

We can determine the truth about a person's values system by identifying how much time, energy, resources, and attention they pay to any area. We spend the majority of our time, thoughts, and energy pursuing our top values. For instance, if you love to "feel good" and drug abuse is your way of numbing out pain, you may spend a lot of time doing drugs or drinking. If you aspire to be a great painter, you will paint and look at art. Each of us is driven in this way, and no one has the right to judge another person's values and needs, nor should they project their values onto another.

When a marriage completes, it is in part because there are not enough similar values between the pair. When this happens, certain feelings, such as not being appreciated, not being an equal, and not being important are spawned from not having our values met, honored, or acknowledged. These feelings are powerful and can in time issue thoughts of divorce. Thoughts of divorce are also fostered because the one or two once-strong and shared values have shifted; usually because they no longer seem necessary or missing. For instance, if a couple agrees that the children come before them and their own emotional needs, and they believe that divorce is bad for children, they will probably stay together, even if their relationship is unfulfilling. They are not really sacrificing, however; they simply value their children more than their emotional happiness. They are still committed to their own highest values in keeping the children in a traditional family unit, rather than having them be children of divorce.

## Journal Exercise:

On page 84 in your *New Divorce Paradigm Journal*, please list what your current top ten values are. They will be in the seven areas of life—financial, familial, spiritual, mental, social, physical, and vocational. Think about children, financial freedom, work, reading, artistry, dance, athletics, golf, health, fitness, spirituality, personal growth, TV, reading, drugs, drinking, or gardening. Remember the ways you spend your time, money, resources, and energy define your current values. You will talk, daydream, and read about, and educate yourself in your values as well.

Next please list the top values and priorities of your children, followed by those of your former spouse.

The reality is that if you can honor and respect the values of your former spouse as well as your own, the way you communicate will change. Your former spouse's values and desires are as important to them as yours are to you. Take some time to discover how your spouse's values benefit you. How do they help you get what you want? The degree to which you link your values to those of your ex and those of your children is the degree to which you can negotiate a fair deal between you.

Now take some time to consider what values changed for each of you that began to move the relationship towards its completion.

Please journal out your findings on page 90 of your *New Divorce Paradigm Journal.*

## Chapter Four

# When Fear Shadows Action

INTEGRITY DIVORCE PRINCIPLE NO. 4

*Energy cannot be created or destroyed;
it can only be transformed.
Therefore, there is nothing missing; there is
just a new form of whatever we need to
manifest in our new life and our destiny.*

## My Journey: Private Thoughts

I innocently believed that it was the desire of
Adam and Eve to include me in the joint parenting
agreement we had reached just five months earlier,
and that was ultimately why I followed them to
Edmonton. To fulfill my role as the girls' mother, I
needed to be sufficiently close geographically, but
Eve was not supportive of my intentions. She and I
had decided from the start that we could set a
precedent and demonstrate that even though
marriages break apart, individuals could create
healthy co-parenting roles. We wanted to set a new
paradigm, or so I thought. Originally, the goal was to
continue to nurture the growth of the children and in
doing so, support Adam and Eve's marriage, and to

blend family dynamics. In hindsight, I should have paid much closer attention to the fact that Eve had my girls call her "mom" just weeks after they had moved in with her and Adam.

In the six months following my relocation to Edmonton, I began to see the hidden agenda that Adam and Eve had had all along. I learned that Eve had become pregnant weeks prior to their request for shared parenting. She had not expected to have children because of reproductive health problems, but when she "miraculously" became pregnant and realized that she was going to be a mother anyway—why not mother all his children?

Eve confessed to me 14 years later that she had deduced that since she was pregnant with one child, she might as well have them all! At first, she wanted to try the shared parenting plan, but within weeks of caring for the girls, and feeling resentful towards me, she and Adam had concluded that they could have the "perfect happy family" if I were not around.

What I learned about Eve's childhood early on in our relationship helped me to understand her actions in regard to my girls. When Eve was 13 years old, her mother had died of a brain hemorrhage. From that time onward, she perceived her mom as missing, unattainable, and unavailable for support. She became very angry with God "for taking her mom away." We had this discussion the first time we met, which was four months after she and Adam began their relationship. I had assured her then that her mom was neither missing nor unavailable for her to talk to, although she would need to use her thoughts, rather than her voice, to communicate with her. She discounted both my suggestions.

For Eve, the perceived "absence" of her mom, which began soon after her mom had died, became an unconscious destructive driving force in her psyche. This perceived "void" set into motion a cosmic dance that would in time transform us all. Remember that anything we do not love, because we cannot see the two sides of it, we will ultimately *create, attract,* or *become.* This is what I call the CAB Principle©; it refers to a universal spiritual law which attracts to us that which we have not loved and appreciated because we did not understand it fully. Therefore, Eve was "destined" to repeat what she did not love, namely her perceived abandonment from her mother.

Consciously, Eve wanted to change the outcome of her mother's "leaving"; she wanted to have her back, or find some replacement for the void. Unconsciously, she wanted to save anyone who in her mind had become abandoned in some form. First was Adam— then my girls. From her perception, I had abandoned them all, so she could rescue them from the pain she had felt when her mother died.

Consequently, what she seared into the girls' little minds was that I was like her mom in that I had left them, but that she could replace me, so that they didn't have to feel what she felt. Since in her perception, her mother had abandoned her, she could "save" the girls from experiencing the pain that she had felt so deeply.

It is important to realize that on a soul level, all these dances were proceeding according to the cosmic plan. I have since come to understand that my girls, Adam, Eve, and I were contracted to do this dance together. The question is, could this dance have been done more caringly? The answer is undoubtedly yes.

Are there as many blessings because it wasn't? The answer, again, is yes. And that is the magnificence of the *Great Orchestrating Design*—God. No matter what we do, we are loved, and so are those who are affected by our choices. The fact that Adam and Eve were destined to care for my girls was predetermined, but that I needed to be excommunicated from their physical lives was not.

I know that both Adam and Eve were reflections of myself; both sides of me—the parts I liked and the parts I saw as bad or shadowed, that I once kept hidden. Also, I know that we were all simply pursuing what we valued—a family life, the healing of some perceived voids, and true love. I am certain that each of us held particular beliefs that we were to experience and learn to love. I see clearly how everything we resisted loving and seeing the order and magnificence in, we created, attracted, or became. And, lastly, how all of us suffered from self-esteem issues, for the same reason we all do: because we didn't really know who we were, or how truly magnificent we already were.

As I reflect back on my story, I remember how, over the six-month period I was to live in Edmonton, a "comedy of tragedies" would dance through my life, which set the stage for the next dance. During the month of November 1985, Eve and I had a volatile hot-and-cold relationship. From the beginning, there had been a strange blending of her wanting my approval and support, and wanting me out of her life. At the time, I was unaware of the reason why she sought my approval. It felt to me like a fatal-attraction relationship. One day, she was pleasant and wanted desperately to be my friend, while the next day, she was feeling abandoned by me and became distant and uncommunicative. I was often on edge and on guard.

On December 22 of the same year, I became violently ill, running dangerously high temperatures, and I fell unconscious for three days. I had contracted the Texas Flu. Adam and Eve ignored my initial pleas for help, and my daughters were told I didn't care about them enough to be with them on Christmas Day, and that they should not expect any Christmas presents from me.

On December 27, after much pleading from me, Adam and Eve brought the girls over to my place. Grateful and exhausted, I prepared a Christmas dinner for them all, and they opened the presents I had purchased. I had asked to have the girls alone to celebrate what was left of the Christmas season; my request was once again denied.

Because Eve did not trust me, and she was afraid that I would run off with the girls, she never permitted me to take all three at the same time. From the day the girls had moved in with her and Adam, I had never had all three children alone with me. In spite of prearranged visits of all three girls, there was always an excuse why I could not take one of them, and most of all not Sara. I was too unsuspecting or naïve to recognize Eve's game.

Fourteen years later, Eve confessed that she had done this because she was so afraid that I would run off with the girls. However, I would not have taken the children from their father, simply because I did not want my children to have to go through the childhood experiences that I had not yet learned to love. The idea of running conjured all sorts of sad memories of an unhappy childhood for me. I simply could not put my girls through a life of running and hiding, because I knew that Eve, more than Adam, would never give up looking for us. Not only because she loved the girls so much, but because she desperately needed to have my role, as both wife and mother, to heal her unconscious wounds. It would take me 14 years to understand all the reasons why.

In the weeks following my illness, my string of misfortune seemed unending, as my car engine seized up and the drive train needed extensive repair. The total repair bills added up to thousands of dollars; it took me four months to pay them off.

My car was confiscated until I could pay off most of the bills. The girls lived in Castle Downs, and I lived in downtown Edmonton, approximately 15 kilometers from their home. I could no longer see them unless I took a taxi to their home. I did so every couple of weeks, but that was not enough for Eve, and she began to resent me yet further. My daily absence was used as "proof" that I didn't want the girls.

Times were tough in Edmonton, ever since I had arrived there in October. I worked at two jobs—a lunch shift Monday to Friday, and from 4 P.M. until closing Monday through Saturday, I was a waitress at the Sidetrack Café and Nightclub. By that point in my cosmic journey, I had become both anorexic and bulimic, with my body weight constantly fluctuating by 20 pounds.

When I wasn't working, I either binge ate, starved myself, smoked cigarettes (to curb my insatiable need to feel satisfied), or pedaled away miles and miles on my exercise bike, which I had put on the balcony, since I would burn more calories pedaling in the

-15°C temperatures. I was consumed with sorrow, guilt, and self-loathing.

By late April, I had decided that the pain and guilt over having given up my children would not end unless I got them back, legally. I felt that if I didn't fight for that opportunity, I would die, emotionally and psychologically, if not physically, since suicide seemed like a good way to finally end the pain.

Psychologically, emotionally, and spiritually, I was crucifying myself for ever having believed Eve and Adam about the joint-parenting scenario. I felt betrayed, and I knew that the only way to survive psychologically and emotionally was to "rise up," but how?

## Regrets, Choices, Hopes, and Dreams

One of the best ways to heal the heart while traveling down the pathway of divorce is to write. So, put pen to paper to unveil your fears in your *New Divorce Paradigm Journal*—be very honest. Now let's take the time to come face to face with some of your fears and your justifications for being hurt and angry. The justifications for being angry listed below are both real and imagined. You will find these questions in *The New Divorce Paradigm Journal* which accompanies this book, beginning on page 36. Please seize the opportunity to grow and become empowered through answering these questions in your Journal now.

- I want a divorce because…
- I am most afraid of getting divorced because of…

- The worst thing that could happen is…
- The benefit of the worst thing happening would be…
- The best thing that could happen is…
- Our child(ren) will benefit from the divorce because…
- Our child(ren) will suffer from the divorce if I…
- And to ease their suffering, I will…
- Our child(ren) will suffer from the divorce if they…
- My finances will change and I will need…
- I am afraid that there will not be enough…

Taking personal responsibility for having a part in the completion of the relationship is also vital. Please bring the following questions, found in your Journal on page 45, into your awareness and answer them:

- What marriage-related grudges am I holding on to?
- Is there something my spouse could do to help me heal from them, so that they will not affect the divorce process as they did the marriage?
- Am I willing to share this information and ask for what I need in order to let my past grudges and resentments go to support the highest outcome for our divorce?

Unowned *anger and blame* cripple the healing process, so it is vital that we expose and become comfortable with our deep feelings of rage, hate, frustration, and blame. Suppressed feelings of anger cause you to "leak" these trapped feelings into other interactions, and this will cause future problems in your communications. It may be helpful for you to pound a pillow, make guttural sounds, or move the angry feelings out through exercise. You may also want to call a friend or therapist to discuss these upsets. The only way out is through!

In your Journal, please complete the following statements, beginning on page 48:

- I resent...
- I'm enraged about...
- I'm exhausted by...
- I can't tolerate...
- I hate...

We divorce in part because we are carrying deep feelings of hurt, loss, and sadness. Let's expose those feelings as well, beginning on page 51:

- I feel terribly sad about...
- I hurt when...
- I am disappointed because...
- I feel invisible when...
- I wanted...
- My heart is broken because...

It is almost impossible to not feel some guilt and responsibility for the divorce. Please complete the following, beginning on page 54:

- I deeply regret...
- I am responsible for...
- I sympathize with you for...
- I did not mean to...
- Please forgive me for...
- I wish...

Healing comes from owning and apologizing for our part in the marriage completion. Please complete the following, beginning on page 59:

- I appreciate that you did…
- I am grateful for…
- I now realize…
- I can forgive…
- I am working on forgiving…
- I value…
- I apologize and feel sorry for…

Even though we are beginning a solo journey in many ways, we will still want to have agreement on certain situations and arrangements that affect both our own life and that of our former spouse. Please complete the following statements on beginning on page 67 in your *New Divorce Paradigm Journal*:

- If we disagree, I want us to…
- When we communicate, I want…
- If I get angry with you, I will…
- When you get angry with me, I would like it if you…
- I hope that…
- If I need help from you, will you…
- I will help…
- I hope…
- I pray for…

Now that you have filled in the above statements, create a Divorce Honor Code to live by.

A template of the Divorce Honor Code can be found on page 74 in your *New Divorce Paradigm Journal* or you can download it free of charge from www.thephoenixcoaching.com. It includes statements that would not apply to couples who do not have children. If this includes you, please substitute statements that would be applicable in your situation.

Invite to your former spouse to complete a Divorce Honor Code as well.

The following needs to be completed only if you and your former spouse had a child or children together. As parents of your child or children, *you do need to agree* about some things. Please complete the following statements beginning on page 75 in your *New Divorce Paradigm Journal* and then discuss them with your former spouse.

- I would love to have our child(ren) _____ percent of the time.
- I would love you to have our child(ren) _____ percent of the time.
- My desire for our child(ren) is…
- I would love us to share weekends _____ percent of the time.
- I would love us to (e.g., share equally) _____ the holidays and special times of the year.
- I (we) will not introduce our child(ren) to people we are dating for ___ months.
- When I (we) begin dating someone new, I (we) will…
- When you begin dating someone new, I would love him/her to…
- Our child(ren) is (are) a priority, so I will…
- When our child(ren) is (are) angry with you, I will…

- I agree to set up a regular time to discuss our child(ren)'s issues every…

The key point to take from this chapter is that whatever we think through and express with our former spouse, we can consciously direct towards the outcomes that support our new life.

To that end, please create a Parental Wish List that reflects your and your spouse's agreement.

A template of the Parental Wish List can be found on page 82 in your *New Divorce Paradigm Journal* or you can download it free of charge from www.thephoenixcoaching.com

Invite your former spouse to complete a Parental Wish List as well.

## Chapter Five

# Evaluations

INTEGRITY DIVORCE PRINCIPLE NO. 5

*Anything and anyone you do not love and appreciate as they are, you will eventually create, attract, or become, until you do love and appreciate them. This is the CAB Principle©.*

## My Journey: Endurance

The following year, 1987, I would travel back and forth to Calgary countless times to meet with my lawyer to prepare for my divorce trial. There also was a new man in my life—Jake—and by October 1987; I was four months pregnant with our son. I was staying in Lethbridge with my dear friend Marsha and driving to Calgary twice a week, anxiously fighting for visitation rights to the girls, who had become extremely hostile as a result of the "programming" against me. Vigilantly, my lawyer and I prepared the evidence for the custody trial ahead.

I sat through discovery after discovery, stunned by the apparent hostility and hatefulness that Adam and Eve displayed towards me. This was coupled with a storybook of lies and deceitful evidence that would not eventually stand up in court. Adam and Eve regularly failed to comply with court-ordered visitations that I had been granted in the six months prior to trial. My only form of recourse had been to call the police to come to their home to enforce the court order, so I could spend some time with my girls. Of course, from the children's standpoint, their perception had been that I was being mean by calling the police against their parents. One of the most extreme accusations made about me during the pre-trial period was an accusation of sexual and physical abuse against Sara, following her having an allergic reaction to blueberries. Eve was often quick to jump to the most outrageous or hurtful of conclusions.

Jake and I were married 18 months after we met. Our whole relationship revolved around my wanting to get my girls back—and his struggle with gambling and alcohol. Our relationship was riddled with hurdles from the start, offering us both tremendous opportunities to grow. Jake needed to earn some quick cash to pay his three years' arrears in income taxes, and I needed big money to pay my divorce lawyer. Individually, we both had unresolved issues with parents and with self-worth. I came into his life in part to help him find his way as an individual apart from his two older brothers, who, for the most part, had "fathered" him since Jake's dad had died when he was young. Jake came into my life to show me that I was still worthy of love, and to financially support me while I focused on regaining a relationship with my girls. It was a gift I am grateful for to this day.

During the last leg before the trial, I was pregnant and unable to work due to the demands of living in

Lethbridge temporarily and preparing for court in Calgary. As I had no income at the time, I was no longer able to pay for the growing legal fees. Heartbroken at the thought that I would have to give up because of monetary issues, I asked for help. Help came graciously, through my lawyer, Karen, who decided it would be a moral injustice to give up, when she knew in her heart that, unless she took action, I would lose all chances of a relationship with my three young children.

Karen pleaded my case to the partners of her firm and offered to do the remainder of the work ahead "pro bono." She was just fresh out of law school and knew in her heart that this was a case worth fighting for. "It was the reason I went into family law to begin with," Karen told me. "Your only responsibility from here on in is to cover the administrative costs incurred by me in order to continue representing you," she said. With tear-filled eyes, I gratefully agreed. Upon completion of this trial, I was made aware that the total cost of the trial had been in excess of $100,000—an amount that was absorbed by many different parties. The portion that I was liable for was a small price to pay for the wisdom I gained, and the love that I experienced from my lawyer.

## The Art of Fair Exchange

As children, my brother and I used to fight over who got to slice up the warm apple pie. In our house, the deal was that whoever cut it must allow the others to have first pick of which piece they wanted. This was my mother's wisdom at its best. My concern, as the "slicer" of the pie, quickly became equality, since I would get the last piece! This same methodology can also be applied to the fair exchange principle, "Whatever you give, you will receive," which is a concept that we would be wise to consider if we want to move through a divorce caringly and fairly.

Regardless of whether we are sharing assets or time with the children, our goal should be to search for what is equal and fair. When it comes to asset division, an evaluation of what size the asset pie is should come long before any claim to a particularly valued piece of property is made. Although it is true that sometimes each person has very different tastes and wants and that therefore, each individual is permitted to have their particular favorite or most valued assets, more often than not, there are some treasures that are equally coveted. When this occurs, we need to be fair. Battles in court can only happen when two people are fighting to have what they want, rather than what would be fair for the other person.

When it comes to being fair with the right to ongoing parenting time, things can get tricky. Often an assumption is made that following a separation, both parents will want or need to have the same amount of parenting time that they had while the marriage was intact. This is an illusion. With the sobering effects that divorce has and the huge emotional impact it brings, it often also heightens our need for emotional closeness to our children.

I have counseled countless people on the fact that after their marriage completes, the parent who was once viewed as not being an active parent may well become much more invested in an active parenting role because of the divorce. Remember we value what we perceive is missing. All too often, I see once distant and hard-working fathers become emotionally enriching dads following the end of their marriage. The spouses of such men can feel betrayed, dumbfounded, and angry. The response I often hear is, "If he had cared about the kids that much before the divorce, we would not be getting one!" My response is always the same. I point out that this is one of the blessings of the divorce dance. I also explain another interesting factor: There is nothing missing. To the degree that one parent will not be as available, the other will be, or another family member will be. The children will get all that they need. The law of life's equilibrating nature will ensure that.

Fair exchange includes the awareness that what we need will always show up through someone or something. The trick is finding the new form that it is arriving through. This can be difficult when we are addicted to things coming only one or two ways. For instance, if I feel I am missing the "spooning" that my husband and I loved to do, the new form in which spooning may come might be from my new cat, who cuddles her body inside of mine.

Many say life is not fair, but I do not subscribe to such a belief. Life is fair, and it gives us gifts in many forms for every investment we make. For example, the gifts I received for going through a heart-wrenching three-year custody battle were wisdom and experience. These are gifts that countless others have also been blessed by! If you asked me to return the experience and all the blessings it brought, you would have a challenge on your hands. I now realize that the gift of Adam's having kept my daughters all those years is ultimately equal to the cost of not having them.

Many of us freeze at the idea of surrendering time with the kids, money, freedoms, and privileges because we believe in loss and gain. Both are illusions. The law of fair exchange always governs us; and we are always being entertained by life to see if we will remember that! We may well lose one form of something we value, but it is only to gain it in another form — one more suitable to our new life.

## Journal Exercise:

Please answer the following questions beginning on page 93 in your *New Divorce Paradigm Journal*:

- What are you most afraid of losing as far as the relationship is concerned?
  - What could be the benefit of losing that?
  - From where or from whom could a new form come?
- What are you most afraid of losing in relation to family?
  - What could be the benefit of losing that?
  - From where or from whom could a new form come?
- What are you most afraid of losing emotionally?
  - What could be the benefit of losing that?
  - From where or from whom could a new form come?
- What are you most afraid of losing financially?
  - What could be the benefit of losing that?
  - From where or from whom could a new form come?

- o Will this "loss" force you to grow into greater independence and freedom?
- What are you most afraid of losing socially?
  - o What could be the benefit of losing that?
  - o From where or from whom could a new form come?
  - o How could this social "loss" serve your vision of a new life?
- What are you most afraid of losing morally?
  - o What could be the benefit of losing that?
  - o From where or from whom could a new form come?
  - o What will a moral "loss" show you about yourself?

*Chapter Six*

# Trials and Tribulations

INTEGRITY DIVORCE PRINCIPLE NO. 6

*You always attract yourself to yourself; you do this so you can own and appreciate all your hidden, unrecognized, and unloved traits. We call this mirroring.*

## My Journey: The Judgment

By December 1987, we finally got to court, and the key assessment to be made was whether or not my girls had been programmed to fear and hate me, and this was appropriately referred to as Parent Alienation Syndrome. Days before the trial, the children announced, "You should just go away—we have a new mommy now, we don't want to be with you."

As a part of the process of determining the truth, my lawyer insisted that we have complete bilateral psychological assessments done, which means assessments of all parental figures and of each child. She chose one of the most respected and knowledgeable psychologists in the city. It took him six weeks to determine, from the extensive visits and psychological tests, who was the better parent. Adam and Eve's lawyer had unilateral assessments done as well, which meant that only the two of them were assessed. I never met with the psychologist they saw in the unilateral assessment, yet in court he discussed, for 20 minutes, my personality traits and what he felt my relationship with my daughters was like.

The evidence from the bilateral assessment was that extensive brainwashing had been going on for years. "The children demonstrated unusually high levels of animosity towards their natural mother," noted the comments in the bilateral report. "Even when working with children who were actually physically abused, I had never seen such angry and unforgiving children," the doctor testified. He spoke about how defensive the girls were of their new "mom," while calling their natural mother by her first name. He said that he found what he saw "greatly disturbing." Then he turned his attention towards the judge and stated that, "strange dynamics were underway between the two mothers." To summarize, he believed that the natural mother was seen as a dangerous threat to the acting stepmother and that he had serious concerns about the stepmother's mental health. He mentioned that the stepmother's mother had died when the stepmother was 13, and felt that there were serious unresolved abandonment issues that she was unconsciously dealing with. In light of the death of the mother, and the unresolved abandonment felt by the stepmother, the doctor indicated that she was unconsciously "rescuing" these little girls in order to heal her own abandonment issue.

Next, the psychologist turned his attention to the father of the children, Adam. He had concluded that he was subservient to the overwhelming emotional needs of his fiancée. It seemed very apparent that it was primarily the stepmother who was the initiator of most of the blending family problems. The psychologist stated that even the father had picked up on some "strange jealousy and envy that she portrayed towards the natural mother." The father had indicated to him that Eve "fluctuated between wanting the natural mother out of their lives, and wanting her friendship and approval, while simultaneously wanting her acknowledgment to show that she had taken over for her when she had 'abandoned' them."

The children were not asked to testify; they were 7, 6, and 4 years old. The days dragged on, with a stream of character witnesses that Adam and Eve had brought in, in order to bash my character. Many of them I did not know. Then, after four heart-wrenching days, it was finally over, and it was my turn to respond.

I took the stand at 9 A.M. and presented my side, which was that I felt cheated by them. All of this had happened because I had trusted in their intention to co-parent. I had never abandoned my girls. The physical evidence of phone bills, a medical report, engine repairs, etc., substantiated the circumstances that I was always committed to being in their life as their mother. I also spoke of the heart-wrenching feelings I had to endure every time I went to their house to see my girls. I shared how hard it was to see that I had been so easily "replaced." I admitted that my emotional, psychological, and physical well-being had taken huge hits in the past three years, but that I felt certain I was well enough to care for the girls. I spoke to the judge and recognized how the times that I was unable to visit the girls, due to extreme circumstances, would have been very hard on Eve and the girls equally. I also reminded of the countless times that I was refused visitation. I admitted that the past years had been tough on all of us, but that I was committed to doing things right now. I suggested that if I were awarded joint custody, I would uphold what was best for the girls, putting the past behind us. I knew I was capable of supporting access to the girls by the four acting parents in their lives. I concluded by asking the judge to do what he felt was best for the girls, to provide stability. If he felt that my girls would do best, in light of all the programming, with my former husband, Adam, then I would sadly comply, provided I had access to them at least a third of the year. I pleaded for his wisdom in what would shape the future of our lives. I was then cross-examined for one-and-a-half hours.

The next person to be cross-examined was Jake, my soon-to-be second husband. He talked about wanting to start a new life with me and our child, whose birth we were anticipating shortly. He said that he was happy to act as a stepfather, but that he couldn't stand the fighting anymore. He spoke about how hard it was on our relationship to go through all of this. Jake said that he could no longer watch me cry and grieve for my girls. He told the judge that the thought of my getting another chance to prove my worthiness as a mother in that I would be able to show my love and devotion to our child, was all that kept him going. He indicated that we would start over in British Columbia. He said that he loved it there, and thought it would be a great place to raise children.

Then my stepdad, Ron, testified. He spoke about the incredibly difficult life that I had had. He said that he didn't know a stronger or more loving mother. He said that he knew that Eve loved the girls, but often wondered about her motive. He indicated that if I had died, she would have been a wonderful fill-in, but this was not the case, and Eve seemed unclear of the appropriate boundaries to her role in the girls' lives. He told the judge that he knew I would never run off with the kids because my childhood had been so painful as a result of child abduction, and that we had spent years hiding from my father and later from social services. He said that if anyone would be able to put the past behind them and do what was most loving for her kids, I would. He apologized for not being there more for me, but stated to the court that he, too, was fighting against his former wife, my mother, for the custody of his son. Ron was the last witness; the trial was finally over, and we awaited judgment.

Affidavit upon affidavit, and stacks of evidence and psychological reports were waiting for the judge to review. Finally, after five days of trial and character-bashing from Adam and Eve's side, and our half-day rebuttal supplying physical evidence for the love and commitment I had always shown the girls, the decision was given.

## Transforming Guilt, Fear, and Judgment

If we are to consider the dualistic world, and the accompanying law of equilibrium, which reveals that all things actually become known by their opposite, i.e., up with down, cold with hot, nice with mean, happy with sad, dark with light, and so on, then fear, guilt, and judgment can be viewed in a whole new and inspiring way.

Let's review time for a moment. Guilt can only occur with a "past" orientation connected to it, and fear is always futuristic or present in time. Both guilt (past) and fear (future) use the present as a starting point. For instance, I cannot feel guilty about something I will do in the future; I can, however, currently feel fear about the impact of doing something future-based which stems from some guilt-arousing action in my past.

For example, I may well have lied to my former spouse about sending the child support payment on the first of the month as I was supposed to, but the guilt I am currently feeling is coming from the past action which I am reclaiming in the present. The fear I feel now for the possible consequences is shadowing my future.

Therefore, we cannot feel guilty about our future, yet we can and often do feel fear because of something we have done in our past which we feel guilty about and now regret. Guilt and fear are often inseparable bedfellows. Find one, and the other is usually not far away.

Guilt and fear are actually founded on a single belief. It is the idea that we can actually be at the effect of an experience or cause an experience which has either more pain than pleasure, or more negative than positive effects, or both. This is impossible, and this belief is an illusion. It cannot happen, nor has it ever happened to anyone, yet we all believe it has. We believe we have had events which offered either more pleasure or more pain because we are literally blinded by the *Warrior's* perceptions within our mind.

All events and experiences are actually equilibrated, since consciousness happens because there is dualism. Consciousness is governed by the same laws as those which create light. The law of opposites and dualism permeates our human condition.

When we undergo a difficult or extremely pleasurable experience, we are focused on that and not on the event or experiences that are opposite to whatever we are focused on. We are always experiencing both happy and sad events and experiences *if we look to see them*. If we don't, they are still occurring; we are just not aware of them. For instance, you are not usually aware of your heart beating unless you focus on it or it is under pressure to beat more rapidly. Our unawareness of what is not overly stimulating is the mind's way of coping. Too many stimuli overwhelm us. Therefore, our ego in its addiction to ups and downs blocks out the other side of an extreme experience, so that we can feel either pleasure or pain. The startling fact is that we do not have to do this, we can *choose* otherwise. To choose equilibrium awareness keeps us stable and victimless—freed from guilt, fear, and regret.

Undoubtedly, the idea that we do at times have more sorrow than happiness is well accepted as not only possible but also true by countless people. The primary reason all experiences are equilibrated is based on science. Interestingly, the laws which govern light and how it "happens" also apply to consciousness itself, since consciousness is itself the "light of the mind." So, without going into a deep explanation about the complex world of quantum physics, we can most simply say that light comes in two forms— particles and waves. And it is from the annihilation or collapse of the two equal yet opposite particles and waves—the electron and positron—that light happens. To say it simply, the particle and anti-particle, which are exact opposites of each other, come together and disappear (collapse), leaving light as the by-product of their union.

The reasonable question that follows is, who decides on whether the particle is measured as either "positive" (the particle) or "negative" (the wave)? We do. We, as the observer, make a judgment, or hold a desire or value, which takes a *once neutral and immeasurable pure potentiality,* which is unseen, and turns it into a "something," making it measurable and manifesting as either a particle or wave, which is seen as "physical," by our judgment. Our assessment of anything being good or bad, hard or soft, positive or negative, is driven by our individual and collective values systems. All values, morals, and beliefs are driven by our desire to be good, better than, safe, powerful, free, or desirable.

Since the moment we think that something is negative or bad in our evaluation, we simultaneously manifest its opposite—something that is "good" in equal measure—we should no longer feel guilt or fear regarding any of the necessary changes that accompany divorce. This may seem shocking, but it is true. Let's consider, in my story, the cross examination that took place in the courtroom just before the judge made his decision about the custody of my girls. Although I did not recognize the "pleasure" side of the experience at the time, I realize now that I had just as much support as challenge, as much pain as pleasure, and as much loss as gain of motherhood that day. My lawyer and her firm, my friend, my stepfather, and my fiancé were all loving, caring, or supportive of me while their lawyer challenged me. The truth is that the judgment that was given that day brought with it both imprisonment and freedom in equal proportions for me.

Again, values are based on voids (the things we view as missing that we want) and adopted beliefs and morals, so by our desires, we shape the world we notice around us.

Since our judgments and evaluations of what is good or bad, and pleasurable or painful, are reflective of our current desires, pain and pleasure are interchangeable. For instance, if I am trying to get into shape and I have been weight lifting and the following day my muscles are burning, it is "good," because the pain is indicative of my gain. If, on the other hand, I am preparing to go dancing all evening and my muscles are burning, those same stiff muscles will be evaluated as "bad," because my flowing body movements, required for dancing, will be compromised by the aching, tight muscles—the pain is then "bad."

All things, people, traits, characteristics, events, and experiences are measured by us in this same way. Whatever makes us feel safe, empowered, and powerful is generally evaluated as "good," while those things or experiences which do the opposite are judged as "bad."

When it comes to divorce, fear and guilt are critical arsenals for the *Warrior* to employ. Guilt is a weapon used by this heartless companion, who hungers for victims. The *Warrior* is not concerned with *who is the victim* as much as it is concerned with there being one—even if it were you! For this reason, guilt is an illusion, often subscribed to, that we must detect and extinguish wherever it is recognized. Therefore, if your spouse has done something to you or the children that you feel only delivered pain, look again and ask, "Where was the support, and where is the pleasure or gift that came partnered to the pain or challenge?" I promise it is there—you only need to look! It may come from either a real or virtual person or through a memory, and it may be connected to another area of your life. For instance, if the challenge came in the parenting arena, the support may come in the social area of your life. The support can come from yourself or from another being either near or far away, but it is a physical law of the universe that any time we are challenged, we are also supported! So, go find the support and give up the guilt. Guilt is a deadly emotional and psychological cancer!

The rooting out of fear and guilt is imperative to the success of a gentle divorce, and each and every decision that is linked to the completion of the relationship must be made with the mindset that both parties have made mistakes, but that those mistakes are not to be used as weapons. Most important of all is the recognition that we must illuminate the guilt we feel towards ourselves by looking closely at the guilt-fostering actions we feel we have undertaken and then find the equalizing benefits that arose and will arise in the future. This is critical work to be done if we are to move through our divorce caringly and fairly.

Since guilt presumes that we can have an experience outside of the law of duality and equilibrium, yet we cannot, there is no one to blame. Further, because we can be "blinded" or unaware of the equilibrium process that stabilizes our life and ensures that the positive which is accompanying the negative will be in perfect proportion, seeking for such positives as we move through a divorce is crucial.

Because we are conditioned to see only one side, we must decide on which team we are playing. We have a choice between the *Warrior's* team of guilt, fear, victimhood, gain, and loss, or the transformational side of the *Teacher*—the side that supports equality, fairness, equilibrium, and transformation, rather than the belief in gain and loss. The guide that we are listening to will elicit either confidence, hope, and optimism, or fear, hate, and pessimism—it is your decision as to which you want to follow.

What is interesting is that we do tend to be able to see both sides of an experience when we look back on the hard times that we have endured. The well-worn statement that hindsight is 20/20 comes to mind. What "life masters" do, but which we often forget, is to hold this hindsight "vision" in the present, towards all upcoming events of their future. You can do this also.

The reality is that, no matter how negative and pain-filled an experience is, there are positives and pleasurable experiences and relationships occurring simultaneously, so look for them. For instance, we can be going through a rocky divorce and get a promotion at work, and therefore get a raise. Our mother may be diagnosed with diabetes, while our child is receiving a scholarship and some much needed self-esteem. I may be losing a life partner and gaining a new and authentic self, which is of equal value to my future. I may be losing a six-figure income and gaining a new best-selling book idea that will make me millions in time. And if we look, we will see that these events were indeed happening simultaneously, without our awareness.

The painful yet inspiring truth is that the impacts of a divorce will most likely breathe sorrow into the hearts of the family, and they will also instill relief, hope, strength, and self-reliance. The reality is that everyone involved will be held in equilibrium. They will be given experiences that are judged as both supportive and challenging, and that will prepare them for their futures. All events and the changing directions that come out of the divorce will ultimately be reflective of their values and dreams to support their destiny.

For instance, recently the daughter of a couple I am working with learned that her parents were divorcing and she would be moving away from her school friends. I helped her to see that that the new house they would move into would be next to the acting school she had yearned to attend. Years later, she may perhaps recognize that the new man who has come into her mother's life is arranging a modeling contract, which may well catapult her into her dream of an acting career!

Here is a profound question to ponder: If no one were guilty, no matter what the experiences were that led to the marriage completion, but rather that each person were being redirected, through circumstances, towards the life they were destined to live, how would getting a divorce feel different for you?

You always attract yourself to yourself; you do this so you can own and appreciate all your hidden, unrecognized, and unloved traits. We call this *mirroring*.

## My Journey: From Obstacles to Understanding

In my testimony, I had asked the judge to do what he felt best for the children—for their best outcome in the future, given all the evidence.

In his statement, the judge reprimanded Adam and Eve for their appalling and so apparent behavior in the courtroom and in the previous years. He then continued by saying he felt that if I lived in Calgary, where the children resided, he would have awarded me the day-to-day care and control. However, because this was not the case, and considering the geographic distance, coupled with the many years of estrangement and parent alienation that the girls had suffered, he felt that it was in their best interest to continue residing with the father, but stated that a very detailed list of access times to the children would be prepared and that if, at any time, access was denied again, he would immediately order the change in custody, care, and control. The judge closed the case, suggesting that I should come back to see him if there were further issues with Adam and Eve. I never did get an opportunity to do this, however, because he retired a year after the case closed.

## Reflections on the "Judgment"

Most of us have the belief that if you are a good person, then only good things should happen to you. And alternatively, if you are a bad person, ultimately bad things will happen to you. From the many difficulties I experienced throughout my life, I learned that this is a self-limiting, judgmental, and mistaken belief. What is good or bad depends on who is discerning it, based upon individual ideals, values, and beliefs.

We tend to become fearful when, though we are comfortable doing the more common dances, we are expected to leap in our learning and become skilled at the intricate steps of a more complex dance—a dance which we feel is painfully hard to learn, but which, if danced by a seasoned master, who demonstrates that it is possible to accomplish, we also marvel at.

We are masters, and we are all here to learn each and every experience, or dance, that reveals love's power. We eventually do all the dances necessary to evolve. As a result of incorporating every step of each of the dances, we will eventually be able to aid others in doing them also; and through our first doing them, followed by integrating them, we will know with certainty, as does the master, the gratitude that is present in their accomplishment.

To the soul, the path that is pursued most diligently is the one that will teach us how to love most fully and honestly. The soul will embark upon the dance floor, which is certain to attract those partners who will most reflect both loved and unloved parts of itself. Magically, then, we will each come to learn that moving in and through love does not mean self-sacrifice; rather it means that the self becomes more expansive, encompassing all our dance partners. Through dances like these, we become truthful enough to see that no one really betrays anyone, but is instead only pursuing what each values and appreciates, just as we do.

Great people—who we all are—need to grow through difficult transformative experiences in order to digest the power and wisdom that these occurrences bring. Once these experiences are integrated, understood, and loved (meaning they are seen and appreciated from both sides, and for all involved), we have the power to transform other individuals' perceptions, too.

*Chapter Seven*

# Transformation

INTEGRITY DIVORCE PRINCIPLE NO. 7

The only thing that is ever lacking from any situation is that which you are unwilling to give to that situation. Most often, this is compassion and pardon.

## Your House—My House

Following a divorce, there will be days when you are feeling sad or angry and are therefore hungry to feed off the struggles within your former spouse's home. You must resist this temptation, however, because your children are the prey for such a hunger. Since we fluctuate between feeling strong and weak as we travel down the road of divorce, the desire to feel bigger at the expense of making the other side feel weaker or smaller can feel irresistible.

Shortly following the separation and divorce, and once the children are moving between two homes, there will be different rules in each house to live by. The children can and will adapt best when they are told it is natural to have different rules in each house. Many fantasize about the idea or belief that we can operate under one set of rules, as was done under the umbrella of a marriage unit and a unified family. With two households, this will not be the case. Although some basic and fundamental guidelines are important and can be adhered to by both parents, such as doing homework, cleaning up after oneself, and proper behaviors, most, if not all, homes will differ in tolerances and values regarding other issues.

Children do grow through a blending of support and challenge, hardness and softness, strictness and lenience, and depending on which house is dominated by either the softer or harder approach, the opposing side will equilibrate these energies.

Children have voices and opinions, wants, and desires, just like adults do. They should ideally be encouraged to express any feelings of upset to the parent they are upset with. Be very strong in this. Children generally want their parents to get together again, and so they unconsciously and consciously create scenarios that force parents to stay connected, whether in a positive or negative way. Telling Mom that Dad is so mean is a way to get Mom talking to Dad. Another common tactic of children of divorce is to say or do things that can keep their parents engaged through fighting one another.

A wise parent will encourage the children to talk to the parent towards whom their upset is directed and will facilitate this. If your relationship with your former spouse is so deteriorated that communication is non-existent, involve a parent co-ordinator to speak with and arrange a meeting between the conflicted child and their parent.

## Transforming the Old into the New

Another issue that slows the healing process after a divorce is the idea that something that is valued is or will be "missing." This is not true as it appears initially. Einstein surmised that energy couldn't be created or destroyed; it could only be transformed. Science has confirmed this to be true. Everything is made up of energy; therefore, everything is under the law of energy dynamics. The impact of the idea that transformation rather than gain or loss of energy occurs is actually alarming.

Since energy cannot be created or destroyed, it would also mean that all parties involved in the division and rearrangement of assets would be equally governed by the transformation because they, too, are made of energy.

Many of us are hypnotized into the belief that when we divorce, we get half of everything, and sometimes not the half we wanted. While it is true that when we get half of everything, the other half that our spouse gets will be gone from your life in "that form," it is equally true that a new form of what they got is simultaneously appearing in your life. Here is an example. Lesley and Lance are getting divorced. They have two kids, and Lesley will have the kids live with her during the week, while Lance will have the kids every weekend.

## Journal Exercise:

You can find the Circle of Finance exercise on page 106 of your *New Divorce Paradigm Journal*.

Here are their assets:

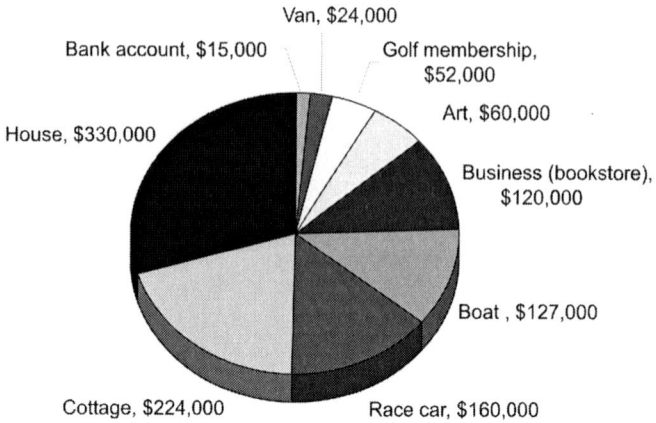

The assets are assessed and equally divided, and both have agreed to who gets what.

| Lesley | | Lance | |
|---|---|---|---|
| House | $330,000 | Business (bookstore) | $120,000 |
| Boat | $127,000 | Race car | $160,000 |
| Art | $60,000 | Cottage | $224,000 |
| Van | $24,000 | Golf membership | $52,000 |
| Bank account | $15,000 | | |
| **Total** | **$556,000** | | **$ 556,000** |

Lesley is angry with Lance because although she agreed to his having the cottage, she misses being able to go to it on weekends. I ask her to identify what about the cottage she feels is missing. She replies, "The cottage itself, the log home, the beautiful bay windows, the view, the hardwood floors, and the indoor hot tub." "Good," I say. "Where do you have a new view that is equally valuable to the one at the cottage?"

Lesley says, "I don't have a new view."

I ask her about the view from her home that she has possibly not noticed. She says, "No, there is no new view."

I ask her what it is about the view that she loves. She replies, "It makes me feel free, alive, and grateful."

"Where are you feeling free now?"

"From the painful marriage."

"What is now occurring that is making you feel alive?"

"My independence, and my new job," Lesley replies.

"What are you most grateful for?"

"Lance's being so fair and reasonable through the divorce, and allowing the kids to be with me all through the work week."

"If I had to compare the value of the old view with the new 'view,' are they equal?" I ask.

Lesley replies, "No. I actually believe my new view is worth more."

"How much more?" I ask. "In dollars and cents?"

Lesley sits still and thinks. "I can say truthfully and with certainty that it is worth the entire loss (transformation) of the cottage. I would rather have what I have now than the log home."

Each of us does throughout our lives transform all things. We decide to sell homes and businesses, cars, and possessions to gather other items or experiences which are more congruent with our current values, desires, and needs. No matter what goes or comes, it is always in our best interest and directed towards our destiny, and sometimes towards a new life richer in growth and opportunity than the one we have outgrown.

## My Journey: Who Is Your Mother?

My relationship with the girls was becoming increasingly strained because Eve was again trying to impose her values and parenting beliefs on me. She regularly called Social Services to report my mothering style and to ask if I was abusing my children, for a myriad of reasons. One of these reasons was that I allowed Joe, my eldest son, to go to the play park, which was in the centre of the condo development we lived in, all by himself.

In all fairness, I do admit that I was a trusting, liberal mom. I was not run by the "what ifs" of life. I had a clear sense of intuition that I listened to and trusted. This drove Eve crazy; she was the polar opposite to me in all her "mother" applications—she represented my unexpressed self, as I represented hers. I did not impose my mothering skills on her, so why did she feel she had to impose hers on me? I asked this question after each call I would receive following my weekend or Wednesday evening visits with the girls.

By September of 1991, I was divorced again, raising my two sons, and I was once again moving. This was a minor move across the road to a lower-income housing complex, where I would live for two years. During this period, I worked, I dated, and I rode the roller coaster of Eve's emotions. The girls were steadily becoming more demanding and judgmental towards me. They were beginning to feel more and more anxious about their visits, because both Adam and Eve were so cold and evasive when they returned.

Because the girls were getting the gears at home for coming to see me, they began to take out their feelings on me. Speaking out to their parents about their feelings of being torn apart was unimaginable, because of the parents' controlling, manipulative, and disciplinary behavior. Adam and Eve had been telling them for years that they needed to decide which parent they wanted, because having both their dad and me freely in their life was out of the question. Eve had been telling them that, if any one of them wanted to live with me, they would have to say goodbye to their other siblings. For my girls, this threat increased the "cost" of living with me. Steadily, they were becoming more and more afraid of challenging these conditions, and the idea of changing homes some day became more and more unthinkable for them.

Soon, Sara, my youngest, no longer came for visits with me, although Emma, my oldest, and Tasha, the middle daughter, still did. Eve always had a different excuse. Sara, who remembered only Eve as her mother, had bonded tightly; she was the easiest of the three girls for Eve to control. Forcing Sara would have only aggravated an already volatile situation. I had long since learned that diplomacy and non-threatening action got me further ahead than did force. I just reminded Sara that I loved her and was there if she wanted to come.

From Sara's perspective, she wanted to make Eve happy, and since Eve would cry as she got the girls ready to visit me, Sara deduced that if she stayed with Eve, she could make her mommy "happier." Gratefully, Eve's tears did not work as well on the other two, Emma and Tasha.

The months that followed became more difficult; I was again losing self-confidence, feeling unlovable and unwanted as I moved from relationship to relationship. All I wanted was a good guy, someone whom I could trust, and someone who saw my goodness and wanted to have a loving relationship. By Christmas of 1992, I realized that I was again losing my girls. Scheduled visits were not being kept. I saw them only about once a month.

That year, it was my turn to have Christmas with the girls. I had not had them on Christmas Day since before they went to live with their dad, in spite of the fact that, according to the decision of the trial judge, I was to have them every other Christmas. In fact, I did not get them for even half of my awarded time. I was too tired to fight in court again, and I knew that the influence Adam and Eve had over the girls was much more psychological than physical. I knew that when push came to shove, the girls would again side with them, so again I surrendered. The impact that Adam and Eve had was shown to me when, on my scheduled Christmas visit, Emma called to say that she and her sisters were staying with Adam and Eve instead. I was heartbroken, but not surprised. On the following Wednesday visit, they uncaringly und unappreciatively tore open the gifts still sitting under the tree. It was not the Christmas I had yearned to have with them.

## Chapter Eight

# Cause and Effect

INTEGRITY DIVORCE PRINCIPLE NO. 8

*Whatever you give,
you will eventually receive.*

Most of us at times think that we are at the effect, rather than the cause, of our life. In particular, we are prone to such reversals within the dynamics of our romantic relationships. We forget, or have never been taught, that we are quite literally living out our core beliefs about people, the world, and ourselves. We are learning this, so that we can become self-actualized masters, and accept *full* responsibility for every aspect and event of our life.

Often, we are oblivious to the fact that the way we treat ourselves will be reflected back to us by our former spouse. The *self* (*Warrior* or *Teacher*) we identify with and establish to guide our relationships will indeed attract very different experiences with varying "dance partners." This is true because the foundations and beliefs held by each of these opposing selves are so different. If we are under the belief that we are unlovable, guilty, deprived, broken, and shadowed, we will attract behaviors from our partner to reflect those beliefs back to us.

Consequently, when we are realigned with our true self—the *Teacher*—we attract that which is congruent with our deeper and authentic identity as being abundant, lovable, charitable, compassionate, and so on. This transfer of identification is itself the shift from listening to the *Warrior* and instead taking counsel from the wise *Teacher*—the transformation from the old into the new paradigm of divorce.

Through the wise internal *Teacher*, we realize that we are destined to *create, attract,* or *become* anything we have not learned to love and appreciate. Relationships can therefore be at times very painful. From this recognition, however, we can learn to understand and appreciate a disliked trait or action in another or within ourselves and to recognize how it facilitates greatness, growth, and opportunity. When we do so, we turn "rejection" into appreciation, which opens the heart to loving and appreciating all of each other and ourselves more fully, and this is congruent with the new divorce paradigm. With this under-standing, our relationships become transformative models for potential soul growth and development.

The traits and qualities we do not love and understand are usually driven by our limited awareness of how what we evaluate as negative simultaneously unfolds the positive. For instance, the perceived stinginess of my mate will initiate my generosity. Further, my evaluation of this trait in him will invite me to see and love it in myself. Although I may perceive him to be stingy in offering up his time, I may realize that I am stingy with lending out my books. As I am wise enough to realize that fear is driving this trait in me and in him, I can decide to realign my belief, making it congruent with my real and abundant self. Once I have done so, I will have a new *self*, which he can "mirror" back to me.

In this model of growth, you will notice that I did not ask him to change in any way, nor was it necessary for me to do so. Instead, I owned that same trait (stinginess) within myself and integrated it into my deeper nature. This integration process is what nurtures us to be what we really are.

Defensiveness is the most common indicator that the *Warrior*, rather than the *Teacher*, is directing the divorce process and the issues between the partners. Defensiveness is a sure sign that cause and effect have been split and reversed. The splitting means that we believe there is a time lag, which establishes a space between what we think and how we experience that thought. This is an illusion the *Warrior* cherishes, because it keeps us "at effect" and powerless to change our lives and relationships.

When we are in contact with our internal *Teacher*, we feel safe, secure, openhearted, open-minded, and empowered to communicate, rather than dictate, our needs and desires. If communication means that we can both speak and hear one another, and thus recognize each other's perceptions and work collectively to find common ground between the parties, then communication becomes an expression of love.

To know that each soul is cause in the relationship, and to be certain that each is in a three-dimensional experience of their core beliefs, is truly freeing. In knowing this, we're free and empowered to co-create any relationship we feel will serve our goal. If we are true to our authentic selves, which the wise *Teacher* always speaks for, our goal will be kindness, compassion, and a new life—and yes, even love.

Consider the following questions:

- What is my goal as it pertains to the divorce process and outcome?
- What am I doing to sabotage my own goal?

## My Journey: Emma Comes Home

By August 1994, Emma was turning 13. One day, she announced to everyone's surprise that she would be moving in with us. I had always said to the girls that, at any time and under any condition, I would take them back if they wanted to come and live with us. Emma took us up on the open-ended offer. Adam and Eve were furious, and I knew that things were going to get ugly as a result of Emma's decision.

Eve called. I could tell by her voice that she definitely was "a woman scorned." She asked if we had, in fact, agreed to Emma's moving in with us. I said that yes, this was fine with Allan and me. Eve and Adam dropped Emma off the next day.

Emma came to me packing a whole lot of rage because her life had been so controlled by Adam and Eve, and five garbage bags full of physical belongings that had been thrown together as a way of sending a message—"You have betrayed us, and so now go!" Emma knew in her heart that it had always been a choice of one house or the other. The choice she had just made came with a considerable price tag, especially the severed relationship with her siblings.

At that particular time, it was a price she was willing to pay.

The next day, Emma called Tasha to see how things were. Tasha told her that Adam and Eve had moved her into Emma's room the same day Emma moved out. Emma asked if Tasha was going to continue coming on weekends. Tasha said no; Sara had not come for months already.

The first month together with Emma was wonderful. I could hardly believe that after all these years, she was back in my arms and back in my life. I was determined to prove to her that I was a great mom. Then, after the second month, Emma began to show her other side more and more frequently. She was rude, cruel with her words, and unkind to her brothers Joe and Jeremy. Soon everyone in the house began to tiptoe so as not to upset her. She was lying, smoking, drinking, and, yes, being a teen. I had no idea how to please her, and I became terrified of getting her angry and seeing her leave again. She had me right where she wanted me.

By the beginning of month five, I was burning out. Emma had refused to phone or visit Adam and Eve or her siblings. Eve would show up at Emma's school, telling the teachers stories about how I was forbidding contact between the homes. Emma was becoming more and more unreasonable, and unmanageable. Then, one day, while she was throwing one of her usual dirty looks at me, Allan snapped.

He told her it was enough, that he was no longer going to allow a 13-year-old to run his house. He said he was appalled at the way she treated me after all the heartbreak he had watched me endure. He said he was fed up with the way she treated her little brothers—bossing them around all the time. Finally, he told her that she would need to change her behavior, or he would take her back to Adam and Eve's house. She heard him, she changed, and I thought things were going to be fine.

## My Journey Continued: Love Sets People Free

In December, Emma finally heeded my urgings to call her other home. Christmas was coming, and she was beginning to miss her sisters and her brother Luke—Adam and Eve's son. She called, and realized that they missed her and wanted her to visit. She said she would think about it. By Christmas, she had made a few calls to them. We had shopped for presents for Tasha, Sara, and Luke, and Emma wondered if I thought it would be okay for her to go on a weekend visit. I assured her that it would be fine, and that we could start to mend feelings slowly.

Emma left on the first weekend of January 1995. She was to be returned at 6 P.M. on Sunday, but did not come home. At seven, I called their house. Adam answered the phone. I asked where Emma was, to which he sarcastically replied, "Here." I asked why she was late. "According to whom?" he answered. "According to Emma," I answered, "and the years of court order time frames." When the girls had come to visit me, I had always taken them home by six on Sunday; in fact, the kids had become terrified if I was late returning them.

Adam told me they were watching a movie, and that he would bring Emma back by 8:30. I agreed. Then Emma came on the phone and asked me if she could bring home a parakeet. I said not that night, but that we would all talk about it as a family, and decide together. "I knew you would say that," she answered, "Mom and Dad said you would say that, too." I knew that things were bad when she said that. In Adam and Eve's home, much of the weekend had been spent comparing households, and they had determined that they had more to offer.

At 8:45 they arrived, all of them—Adam, Eve, Tasha, Emma, and Luke. Eve got out of the van. By then, Allan was extremely frustrated about their childish behavior. He came out of the house with his voice raised, telling them that solutions needed to be found. Eve began screaming at him about his being one of a long lineup of guys I had gone through. He told her to shut up and said that she and Adam needed to act like adults when moving kids between homes. Adam yelled out, "There won't be any more moves between homes!" He said that Emma would be staying with them.

I remained calm and collected; I knew that force was not going to work with Adam and Eve. I walked towards the van and asked Emma to come into the house with me. Eve locked the van door and told her to stay in the van. All the children were hysterical and yelling at me—telling me that they never wanted to see me again. For ten minutes, I calmly pleaded with Emma to just come into the house with me. She did nothing—her eyes said, "I want to come," while her actions said, "I can't."

Eve was filled with rage, pushing me, and telling me that it was too late—Emma was staying with them. Adam stayed by the van, yelling over the roof. I sent Allan inside, telling him this was not the way to deal with things; he flew up his hands and went into the house. There was a lot of swearing; the incident reminded me of my childhood days, when I would watch my parents go into similar fits of rage. Eve was just like my mother—a grandstander. The last thing you do with them is play into their drama. I knew this, but Allan didn't. Eventually, they drove away. In my heart, I knew that Emma was gone, again.

A couple of hours later, I called their house to speak with Emma. I wanted to go and pick her up. Adam answered, and he told me that he would make sure I never saw or spoke with the children again.

I called Emma the next day while Adam was at work, and I told her I would do anything to get her back if she wanted to live with me. She said no; she and Tasha asked me to get out of their lives and leave them alone.

I called again a few days later; they said the same thing over again. My heart bled with pain. I asked Emma if she wanted me to pack up her room and return her belongings; she said yes. I complied and surrendered again. Packing up her room for a second time was unbearable. Allan was glad she was gone, and so were the boys. No one missed her but I.

I prayed for guidance; and the *Teacher* answered, "You could teach Eve what you know about love. You could help her see that the past is overlooked by love."

"No way. Get someone else to help her. I will pray for her and no more," was my response.

A week after the incident in the driveway, the local police department called. Eve had filed aggravated assault charges against Allan, and we were asked to go to the police station and write out a statement that would later become evidence to be used in court.

We did what they asked and hired a lawyer. The statements that were entering into evidence had been written by Adam and Eve and all four children. No two stories matched up—they couldn't, because the event had never occurred. The police officer said that when there is such a dramatic discrepancy between statements, a trial date is automatically set.

Allan was mortified; he regularly traveled to the USA on business, and if he would, in fact, be found guilty of aggravated assault, he would have a criminal record and be forbidden to enter other countries.

After Emma had left, I had thought about all the perceived injustice I had encountered through Adam and Eve; I had spent hours thinking about it, and I just couldn't stand by and do nothing. I asked Allan if he would support me in fighting to get Emma back; he said no. "And if you fight for that, you will have to go," he said as he pointed to the door.

I plummeted into a quiet despair, unable to discuss my feelings with anyone. A few days later, I vigilantly turned back to what gave me strength—*A Course in Miracles*. Allan was both angry and frustrated with the alleged charges laid against him, and we began to grow apart.

Weeks passed, and things became increasingly hostile between Allan and me. I had become resigned to the fact that our relationship was never going to work because he so resisted my children's place in my life and my deeply committed spiritual life. The idea of leaving the relationship was becoming a reality faster than either Allan or I realized.

For the next two weeks, I cried and grieved for Allan's and my lost love. Allan seemed unfeeling and unimpressed with my wailing, but he did not realize that with every tear I shed, I was getting closer to leaving the relationship.

*Chapter Nine*

# Dealing with Conflict

INTEGRITY DIVORCE PRINCIPLE NO. 9

---

*Our need to be right is driven by our immature ego, while our mature spirit prefers being happy over being right.*

---

Many of us jump to the conclusion that if we have to discuss a sensitive issue, it is destined to become a conflict. This need not be so. Since we are essentially committed to our values and not to one another, conversations that keep this fact at their foundation remain open-ended rather than closed and defended.

Conflicts occur because no two people have the same values system. Sparks fly when someone does not hold our values in the same regard as we do. For instance, one of my top values is reliability, but this is not a value that my second husband holds as it applies to our boys—in this area of life he prefers a more let's-see-what-happens attitude. He is reliable when it comes to being at work on time.

He and I are prone to argument only if I project my value of reliability onto him. And although I used to do this, I have grown wiser over the years, which has calmed our relationship significantly. In dealing with him today, I always have a backup plan for his not following through on the day that a meeting is scheduled between him and our sons. Our boys also know that what Dad said would happen may, in fact, not happen. This has at times been difficult for them, but it has also seasoned them in knowing that some people live by structure and some do not. The great news is, our boys have the wonderful privilege of having two parents with opposing value systems, which does prepare them for meeting a wide range of people and coping with others' values.

Many people may feel that it would be better or *right* that a person be reliable and also that we as parents do need to set the example of *right* behavior and actions. However true these opinions may be for some, it is this attitude which causes conflicts to occur. When we project onto another person a discipline or way of behaving, we are, in fact, judging them as less than ourselves. This judgment always causes friction and defensive, closed-off responses.

Consequently, conflict in relationships is inescapable, since we all feel afraid at times, and superior in other moments. We become afraid and sometimes act in a self-righteous fashion whenever we perceive something we value as being in threat of being taken away. When we are hijacked by unrecognized feelings of fear, we do not think; we react, and sometimes we begin making demands. *When someone in this state of mind approaches you,* acknowledge his or her needs and desires *first,* before sharing your own need. This first step is critical to calming the situation and opening a platform for discussion. Once the irritated person feels heard, we can begin a discussion aimed at a win-win outcome for all, based upon the different values of each party.

Another powerful conversational tool which facilitates conflict resolution, or calming stress, is called *reflecting*. To reflect back to an individual what you have heard them say helps them to hear themselves and to feel heard and noticed. When we are under stress, many of us become less able to hear and to think things through clearly. Having someone repeat back to us what they have heard us say allows us some reflection time and an opportunity to state our case differently, or even apologize if we have been abrupt.

Apologies are powerful healing agents for bruised *Warriors*. Do make use of them. Conflicts can be calmed dramatically by admitting one's fears to another and acknowledging that we are afraid of losing something dear to us. Fear ignites our fight-or-flight mechanism, which often causes us to become either cruel and defensive, or to shut down into silence (stonewalling). Neither defense will work, and both are reflective of emotional immaturity. Emotionally mature people admit their mistakes, as this wards off the *Warrior's* demands to be better or right. Emotionally mature individuals instead allow the *Teacher* to lead through mutual respect and the acknowledgment that both people's values and needs count.

## Communication

Everyone knows that communication is vital for ensuring a functional relationship. But what constitutes real communication? I believe that true communication only occurs when we can share our thoughts and feel heard, while being received with all the feelings our perceptions cause to surface, regardless of their validity or origination. When we do not feel safe and received, communication, whether verbal or nonverbal, becomes eclipsed, and will in time recede into resentment. Most of the communication that takes place between people is, in fact, nonverbal; it happens on a thought and energy level. Understanding and learning to listen for the differing thought processes that accompany both communication enhancement and communication breakdown are important steps in creating healthy relationships.

As has been introduced, we are the decision maker who is "courted" by two very different guides. One is the mature and wise *Teacher*, whose identity is inclusive in being and who directs thoughts and action equating with an authentic-self orientation. The *Teacher* believes that all people deserve care, understanding, and compassion. Therefore, the *Teacher* fosters thoughts and actions congruent with being present and available, and being a patient listener. Opposing the *Teacher* is the immature *Warrior*, who is self-absorbed, defensive, afraid, and autonomous in nature. This is a wounded-self-image based on the beliefs in limit and loss. The *Warrior* dwells either in the past, which is based on guilt, or in the future, which is often based on fear; it is an alien to the present, where effective and empowering conversations occur.

## Surrendering the Ego-Self

In conversations, there are two sides to the thought process that evokes the words we say. On one side of the conversation model are ideas, beliefs, and orientations that facilitate strength; and on the other side are ideas, beliefs, and assumptions that give rise to weakness. The weakness side is sourced by the *Warrior*, who fosters an attitude of presumed fear or loss, and most often both. In contrast, the strength side is authored by the wise *Teacher*, who always infers a position of confidence and attitude of abundance, which foster positive sharing and the ability to negotiate. Having the two sides at work establishes an opportunity to identify and shed away our fear- and lack-sourced ego identities, thus revealing our true abundant selves. This transfer is accomplished through choosing communication based on mutual respect, equanimity, and equality, rather than fear, autonomy, and powerlessness.

The "strength" side is connected to our authentic self. It nurtures unity-orientated recognition and empowerment. Conversely, on the opposite side of the model, is the ego-orientated thought process, which focuses on self-absorption and weakness. As we converse, there is a common and natural movement between the two identities we embrace— the authentic self, the wise *Teacher*, and the ego-self, the defended *Warrior*. These opposing selves can be recognized in the language that we use when we speak—how we communicate—particularly in our tone of voice, energy, and body language.

Defensiveness in tone or action is a sure sign that the speaker is identifying with the *Warrior* instead of the *Teacher*, and their language will mirror that. Consequently, "*Warrior*" communication will become ineffective, because it will be positional and defensive, and the listener will likely feel their values are being threatened. The listener will then become increasingly unable to hear the message being offered, since egos (defenses) usually employ other egos into action, so the listener is planning defenses instead of just listening.

The previously calm listener, who was initially in contact with their authentic self, and thus able to hear the speaker's message, will become seduced into action if they succumb to the *Warrior's* invitation. Next, the listener will begin to plot their defense to protect whatever they perceive to be threatened by the speaker. While the listener is planning their defense, they move out of the present moment and become "deaf" rather than listen, understand the speaker's concerns, and then negotiate a win-win outcome for each person. This cyclical and often downward spiraling conversation model could have been suspended if the listener would have allowed the speaker to share *all* their feelings and concerns without becoming defensive and reacting, and instead had listened and acknowledged what they heard.

Since each self speaks from differing ideologies— either fear or compassion—yet wishes to express itself in order to feel heard and appreciated, we can train ourselves to hear with "whom" (the *Warrior* or the *Teacher*) we are speaking at any given time in our conversation. Accordingly, if we wish to encourage the recovery of the authentic self, we need to learn the art of identifying each self as it emerges in both our spouse and ourselves.

Both personal and soul growth is synonymous with the surrendering of the partners' egos. Therefore, to enhance conversation and create true communication, it is imperative to understand the *Warrior's need to be right*, its desire to blame others, its obsession with control, and its fixation with being autonomous and intensely defensive. Defensiveness erupts whenever we feel exposed, revealing our unloved parts and behaviors, and our young emotional self. This emotional "child" that we all have within us has formulated certain beliefs, based on its limited awareness or perceptions. In short, the child-self is terrified of being wrong and being abandoned or rejected. It is encouraging to know that we can learn to speak in ways that nurture the authentic rather than the wounded ego persona in one another. This is the goal towards which we need to work.

When we identify ourselves as the micro-self, the *Warrior*, we are self-absorbed, limited, and defensive, and in this condition we cannot communicate—we can only become withdrawn, and dictate or humiliate. And in this state of being, we can't fully hear the other person; we can only extract limited information—that which supports us in our idea of being victimized and powerless.

When we are aligned with our macro-self, the *Teacher*, however, we are able to hear fully, because we are in a state of authentic power. From this position, we are listening to our partner with compassion and with the recognition that everything they are saying is also true for us in some area of our life. We are listening for our own fears and apprehensions, acknowledging the sameness between our partner and us, rather than trying to be better than them. It is fair to say, then, that equality is a foundational brick of communication.

Since the macro-self is our natural state of being, we strive in our conversations to elicit this macro-self from our spouse in hopes of healing the joint wounds that we share. To transform our relationships, we bring into the open all the ideas, memories, fears, and hurts that sustain the *Warrior's* identities, in order to enable their transformation from fear and autonomy to compassion and inclusiveness. When we hear our former spouse conversing through the ego identity, we first acknowledge how they must be feeling by repeating back to them what they just said. We continue to do this until they can "hear themselves" and recognize which self is directing their words. We do this in an attitude of caring and understanding with the intention of moving the conversation forward.

In truth, we always yearn to be in contact with our authentic self. So, if we are patient because we are certain that our mate is searching for, and has access to, their authentic self, we become conduits of transformation. From doing this mirroring work, we realize that we, too, are being given an opportunity to support our authentic self. Therefore, gratitude, rather than the resentment that often accompanies a breakdown in communication, emerges within our being. With our shift in awareness and the ownership of our macro-self, disempowered language swiftly shifts to words that reflect empowerment, appreciation, and love.

As the listener within the conversation, we have a crucial function, and one which I believe to be the most important work framing the transformative model of communication. It is imperative for the listener to hold an attitude of *certainty*. When we find ourselves in a situation where communication has shut down, our function is to hold in mind with certainty that our partner is spirit, not ego, and that their essence is innocence rather than guilt. When conversations get "bumpy," it is vital that we recognize that unconscious withdrawal from communication is always directed by the ego—the wounded and emotionally immature self. Subsequently, an invitation to our former spouse to return to the conversation once they are feeling safe and completely received with all their emotions (positive and negative) can be liberating for the divorcing couple. If we truly want honest communication, we will also need to receive our partner's shadow sides, emanating from the fears they are wrestling with. We do so, knowing that we, too, have a shadow side that we want to have heard and embraced.

From this position, we can ask our spouse questions that nurture their identification with their authentic self, rather than their ego-self. We can ask questions such as: Do you want to talk with me so that we can understand each other's concerns? Are you feeling empowered right now or powerless? What are you afraid of losing, and can I help you to reclaim it? What can I do to support your feeling safe? Would saying I am sorry help? Can you try to remember that the past does not have to dictate how you want to feel now?

Each of these questions provides an opportuneity to reclaim birthrights such as peace of mind, appreciation, gratitude, power, freedom, expansiveness, and the full encompassment of our authentic selves.

Communication is synonymous with caring. Communication is an act of union, offered to maintain equality. Everything stems from thought, and all things in form began as a thought and must be sustained by a thought.* If the thought (a belief or desire) is abandoned because we no longer believe it to be true, the form will disappear. Surrender the belief in victimization, and you will no longer attract it into your experience. The "extension" attributes of thought are worth pondering seriously. When an idea is shared, all of it remains with the giver, even though all of it is also given away. Thus, each time we share an idea, we increase it in doing so. If we share the idea of a new form of partnership through the divorce, it will increase each time another individual adopts the paradigm as congruent with their heart's desire.

The law of giving and receiving states that both actions are the same in value and will produce gain for both giver and receiver. All ideas are governed by this law, which applies to thoughts that are natural expressions of our true self, as well as those that are not. In particular, we need to recognize that thoughts that are derived from the ego's desire for specialness (autonomy, guilt, shame, loss, fear, being better than, being right) increase with sharing as well, so diligence

---

* Please refer to my book *Rediscovering Your Authentic Self* for more information on this topic.

in rethinking such fear-orientated thoughts is critical in minimizing communication breakdown.

When we consider ourselves to be special—the ego; the *Warrior*; the more important partner—we create a relationship that supports that "special" self, and our conversations move away from macro-self recognition and empowerment to micro-self, self-absorption, and weakness. In that state, we are defensive, shut down, and, more often than not, become deaf to the feelings and position of our former mate.

We are always communicating, even when we are not verbalizing, because mind is shared by all of humanity. The fear and unrest that arise from the idea of sharing one mind are indicative of the deeply buried feelings of guilt we hold in our consciousness. Guilt arose when we thought we could turn away from love by adopting the idea of specialness. Subsequently, we have learned to connect the idea of sharing one mind with that of transparency. Since we do not want the hidden thoughts produced by the *Warrior* to be known to others, and because the ego tells us that there is a wretched guilt within us for choosing specialness over love and private thoughts over transparent unified ones, the open sharing of our mind is then associated with vulnerability, which in *Warrior* terms means powerlessness and weakness. The ego mind then deduces that transparency of mind implies the exposing of the self that we authentically are. Because we could not, nor ever actually did, usurp love, our natural being remains intact. The ego is indeed afraid of our true loving radiance, and it knows that when we find this authentic self in ourselves and in each other, the ego will cease to exist. It is for this reason that it maintains the urgency for us to keep private thoughts alive. In so doing, however, we sustain special rather than transformational relationships.

Transparent communication is like a light that illuminates the darkness. Darkness simply vanishes into the nothingness from which it arose. The *Warrior* is not interested in any conversation that has as its goal the abolishment of guilt and the reinstatement of innocence; however, the authentic self within you certainly is.

The *Warrior* whispers that there are horrid facets in our nature that must remain hidden. It instills within us the belief that if our partners saw or knew of these thoughts, they would run away in disgust. It warns us to keep a part of us away, especially any part that would expose us as being vulnerable. In our conversations, we are directed to never expose our mistakes or ego-orientated words and actions, since they will perpetuate the already heavy burden of guilt we are carrying. By listening to the whispers of the *Warrior* and by keeping private thoughts, we sabotage the awareness of the unassailable innocence we share.

Empowering conversations, on the other hand, are based on a shared innocence and the mutual desire to expose and heal all thoughts and perceptions based on fear, lack, or loss. The discussions are directed by the wise *Teacher*, not the *Warrior*, and are customized to reveal magnificence, not limit or loss. In a transformational relationship, neither party wishes to blame the other for difficulties they are enduring together. Rather, each person identifies the ways in which the situation can be used to advance their soul growth, since both realize that they are indeed reflections of one another. From this perspective, all healing work is mutually beneficial, and is looked forward to, rather than avoided.

Now let's return to my story to discover the transformation that occurred in my relationship with Allan.

## My Journey: Reconciliation

Allan and I had lived apart for exactly two months when I saw him one day at one of my sons' soccer games, which Allan had continued to attend because he had become so connected with the children. He said, "I want to thank you for helping me." I was puzzled, and he said, "I found God, and I now know how important it is to know God, individually." He had changed, and so had I. I silently wondered if we could begin again.

I repeatedly explained to him that, since spirituality was my top value, I felt closer to those who supported it and felt distanced by those who didn't. Eventually he, too, realized that I was committed not to a person, but to my highest value—pursuing God. Over the following months, Allan grew in his understanding of this truth, and in March 1995, we were married.

## Journal Exercise:

Please answer the following questions beginning on page 111 in your *New Divorce Paradigm Journal*:

- What are the most difficult topics or issues to discuss with my former spouse?
- I am most afraid to discuss these because…

*Chapter Ten*

# Kids and Dating

INTEGRITY DIVORCE PRINCIPLE NO. 10

*Your thoughts become your experience, so that you can awaken to the power of your beliefs—both the known and the unrecognized ones.*

Through the many years that I have worked with children of divorce, I have learned that they need time to heal following their parents' separation. Unconsciously and often consciously, they want their parents to get back together. In part, I think the pull for reunion comes from the strong and ancient family archetype that we are all "plugged" into. Although we are creating a new form of the family archetype, one that includes additional members, the old and traditional model still has a hold on our consciousness and even our hearts.

For this reason, introducing a new person you are serious about into the now split traditional family unit is a process that should be undertaken gently. Children do not really want a different family unit; they want what they know, feel safe within, and understand. Even if the nuclear family was highly conflicted or was stressful because of drug and alcohol abuse by one or both parents, it was an environment they had learned to live within. Kids, like adults, prefer the known to the unknown, and a new person is unknown to them.

Kids also feel very tenuous about how to like, let alone love, a new stranger. They also undergo deep feelings of guilt and betrayal towards their "replaced" parent if the child genuinely does like or love the new member who is joining the family.

Dating and telephone calls with new relationships should be done discreetly. Most kids feel they want about six months to settle into their new way of living before they are introduced to anyone new. Some kids have requested a full year.

Following the six months to one year passage of time, your children should be invited to meet the new love in your life, not told they are going to. Of course, children under the age of four are generally not given such a choice, but rather should be "gentled" into a first encounter, which could involve doing something they love to do, such as play time at the park. Older kids may want to go bowling, skating, or seeing a movie; whatever is decided on, do make it fun. The first meeting between your kids and your new love needs to be geared towards the kids' wants, not yours.

Although it is understandable that when we are in the throws of a new and rewarding relationship and all the "butterflies" of excitement that come with it, we expect our kids to feel as we do about the new love, they generally will not. They unconsciously view this new person as the intruder, and sometimes as the cause of their parents' divorce. So when it comes to dating, go slow, ask the children lots of questions about how they feel about a new person coming into your life. Recognize their feelings, and don't try to override them with logic or your reasoning. Just listen and acknowledge that you hear and understand their concerns and wishes. Let them know that their feelings and opinions count. Do this before you start dating. Kids really do want their parents to be happy, and they do understand your desire for a mate; they just need time to adjust, in their hearts and minds, to the new situation.

Another support for the kids is to allow them to not like your new partner. Although in a perfect world, everyone would just love and welcome everyone else, this is not usually the case. The characteristics and traits in another person can rub us the wrong way, and if this is happening between your child or your children and your new partner, allow it. Be compassionate to dislikes; don't try too hard to have them like each other. Great relationships occur naturally and develop slowly over time. Go slowly. Giving kids space to not like someone often works in the opposite direction.

Remember, kids, like adults, have created a model of what an ideal parent should be. They have also created, or will be creating, an ideal image of a stepparent. They will measure any prospective partner to that standard and discard those who do not measure up, so talk about this fantasized ideal and get them looking to see what the disadvantage would be of having this "perfect' person in their life. Those whom we idolize we will eventually grow to hate; seeing another person for both their strengths and weaknesses is what we are striving towards.

In the opinion of many professionals, all dating should be kept quiet and discreet until the kids are ready to welcome new people into their lives. Some kids say they will never want their parents to date. However, this is said from a fearful state and is not really based on a true feeling. If your child is still absolutely unwilling to welcome new people in after 18 months following the divorce, have them speak with a counselor. It is likely that there are much deeper emotional wounds festering that need to be explored and healed.

Please review the following questions beginning on page 76 of your *New Divorce Paradigm Journal*:

- I (we) will not introduce our child(ren) to people I am (we are) dating for _____ months.
- When I (we) begin dating someone new, I (we) will...
- When you begin dating someone, I would love him/her to...

## Chapter Eleven

# Love and Endurance

INTEGRITY DIVORCE PRINCIPLE NO. 11

*Growth, wisdom, and strength come from a blending of support and challenge. Welcome both.*

## My Journey: The Assault Trial

It was 1996, and almost a year had passed before we went to trial in the assault charges that Eve had laid against Allan. I had not seen or spoken with the children since the alleged incident on the night that Emma left. We had asked for a plea bargain several times in order to spare the children from going to court. We knew it was all a lie, and we did not want the children to be cross-examined and found caught up in lies. Each time, our offer was denied.

On the morning of the trial, Emma, Tasha, Adam, and Eve were there. The crown prosecutor pulled our attorney aside and asked for a plea bargain. She said that she had met with Eve earlier and felt that she was both emotionally and psychologically unstable. We accepted the offer to have a peace bond put in place, which meant that Allan was not permitted to knowingly be within a two-kilometer proximity of Eve.

## My Journey Continued: For Love or Money

Following the trial, 18 long months passed before I worked up the courage to call the girls to see if I could have a dinner visit with them. I was overjoyed when my request was granted. During the visit, many questions about our situation and the previous years were asked and answered. I felt that the visit was successful and that it offered hope for building a better relationship between the girls and me. Apparently, the visit was perceived in a positive light by the girls as well, because Adam and Eve subsequently became very threatened by the possibility of our having a healed relationship, and they denied me all further access to the girls.

I prayed for direction and an answer; the *Teacher* replied, "Write Eve a letter and teach her that love transcends fear, teach her the Course principles; teach her that the past does not have to run the present or future." I refused. "Get someone else to teach her; I can't believe you want me, of all people, to help her— no way!"

A few months later, I hired a lawyer and began legal proceedings to enforce the visitation right that I had been awarded ten years earlier. The request was received at the court, and an order was issued to uphold the interim access until the trial. We made a request for an assessment of the family dynamics; it, too, was granted.

Shortly thereafter, we received a request for our financial records from Adam and Eve's attorney—they were suing for child support, requesting $600 per child a month. In addition, they were requesting the court to take away all previously awarded visitation and custody rights.

The first issue for me to attend to was to have an independent assessment done to prove that the girls suffered from Parent Alienation Syndrome.

Allan and I went to see Linda, a well-respected professional specializing in Parent Alienation Syndrome. She listened to our concerns and then met with Adam and Eve.

She later reported that she believed our situation to be an extreme case of this syndrome, but felt that with the age of the children—Emma (15), Tasha (14), and Sara (12)—the relationship was reparable, with appropriate counseling.

It was October, the month of Tasha's birthday, and I wanted her to have a gift from me. I gave Linda a purse with a note, earrings, and $40, to give to Tasha. The note reminded her that, no matter what, I loved her. I wasn't sure what things she liked, and so I thought some money would allow her to buy what she wanted. In the note, I also told her that anytime she wanted to call, she could.

Adam and Eve refused to continue seeing Linda, and the children refused to go as well. My lawyer and I discussed the issue and conceded that, even with the court order, given the girls' ages, they could not be forced to "listen" to the therapist. We surrendered and awaited the child support hearing.

I prayed that night, and asked for guidance. My inner voice directed me to write a letter explaining the

Course principles. I refused, replying, "She is never going to listen to me; get someone else to teach her."

Affidavits moved frequently between the two sides. Adam and Eve's lawyer, Mick, was requesting financial income statements and previous tax reports for Allan. My attorney, Philip, denied the request based on the fact that Allan had no financial responsibility to the girls.

Philip was a well-seasoned family lawyer; he knew the laws pertaining to support and was almost certain that Allan's income would have no bearing on the requested child support payments. As it turned out, he was right!

We were preparing to enter the courtroom, when Mick walked over. He handed me the purse I had bought for Tasha. I felt sick, and when I looked inside, everything I had put there was still in it. Mick said that Tasha thought of it as a bribe. He suddenly seemed to realize just how hurtful it was for me to have to take it back. I walked into the courtroom with my heart broken, and feeling abandoned.

I sat alone on my side of the courtroom; Adam and Eve sat with a cheering crowd as usual. I was a seasoned courtroom listener; I prayed, "May Thy will be done."

First, Mick presented his case to the judge, who was an attractive, well-polished woman. I sensed an inner wisdom from her and humble self-appreciation. I hoped that her gender would be in my favor. I had no idea if she had children of her own, or if she could relate to what really was at the root of Adam and Eve's request.

Mick was busy flinging out untruths and was quite apparently charged up about our refusal to submit exact income figures. We did disclose, however, that Allan's income exceeded $100,000 per year, which seemed to aggravate him even further. Mick tried every approach to convince the judge that Allan's income had to be considered in their request for $1,800 a month child support, arrears payment of a year, plus all legal fees.

The judge listened, no sign of which way she was swaying, although she did tell Mick flat out that Allan's income had no bearing in this case. He attempted a rebuttal; she hushed him, and sternly told him his request was ludicrous.

Philip approached, and told my story. The judge showed no emotion; she repeatedly looked me in the eye. She asked what my income was; Philip told her that it was $600 per month, from child support from the father of my two sons. This monthly income was not reliable because my former husband often missed payments and was several thousand dollars in arrears.

The judge asked Philip about the relationship I had with my former husband. He told her it was a good relationship, without access problems of any kind. He mentioned that, although the boys' father was in arrears in child support payments, I never hindered the relationship between my sons and their father. Next, the judge asked if Allan had any children. Philip replied no, but said that he definitely believed that Allan had assumed the role of father to my two sons. He explained that Allan's level of commitment was in fact so great that, as part of the divorce agreement between Jake and me, he had legally assumed full financial responsibility for the boys.

Next, the judge asked why I did not currently work outside the home. Philip told her that I had been a working single mother for most of the time since my sons' births, but that now, as a stay-at-home mom, I volunteered at the school an average of three days a week. He continued by stating that Allan and I owned a large acreage, and that I cared for that also. He added that I was planning to go back to school and pursue a degree in psychology the following year.

The unusual thing about their conversation was that they talked about me as if I weren't there. I got a clear feeling that the judge was busy assessing my character. When she asked me to rise and to tell her why I wanted to be a psychologist, I replied that I loved people and I loved understanding how the mind works. I told her that I studied spirituality and loved to counsel. She replied, "Your life experience would have had something to do with your desire, I am sure." I did not reply, but she said, "Thank you; you may sit down."

Next, she said she needed a 15-minute break, after which she would give us the verdict. When she returned, she said that she had investigated whether or not she could deny the request for child support completely. She said that Alberta law required all parents to make a minimum payment of $100 per child to the day-to-day caregiver.

She said she was appalled by this couple's request, and denied them costs. She said that since they had already destroyed the relationship between the girls and their mother, there was no point in securing visitation access. She looked at me caringly and said, "I am sorry for what they have done. My prayer is that the monthly support payment of $300 until they each reach the age of 18 will show your children in some fashion that you contributed to their life." She said that she was required by law to order a minimum of six months' arrears payments, and that I would have to pay those also. Next, she addressed the application by Adam and Eve that my request for legal custody be removed from the records. She denied that request, hoping that the girls would one day understand that the court had clearly seen the parent alienation that had occurred, and did not want to support Adam and Eve's decision to remove me from the girls' lives. The judge told me, "They will always be your children in your heart. I hope that one day, your girls will see what has happened here."

I sat breathlessly—she felt that she had done all she could to help enforce justice. I felt once again betrayed by the system.

## New Beginnings

Clearly, a divorce causes us to reshape and to redirect our lives. We will have a barrage of questions to decide upon. We need some time and space and often some counsel or coaching to get through the maze. What is most critical at this time in your transition is that you remain open to the possibility that the choices you make today are not choices that need to last forever. They are choices that are moving you towards your next step or phase.

At this time, you will be doing some powerfully transformational questioning.

Please answer these questions beginning on page 123 of your *New Divorce Paradigm Journal:*

- Who am I?
- What have I been neglecting about my needs and wants?
- What is most important for our child(ren)?
- What is my goal as it pertains to the divorce process and outcome?
- What am I doing to sabotage my own goals?
- What are my goals, professionally, personally, as a parent, financially, spiritually, and romantically?
- What career changes can I make or are necessary for me to reach my goals?
- What do my extended family members need most?
- Where shall I live, and in what style of housing?

The answers to these questions may well change depending upon the day and mood you are in. Ask these questions repeatedly and keep journaling your answers.

## Chapter Twelve

# Apologies Heal

INTEGRITY DIVORCE PRINCIPLE NO. 12

*Apologies heal.*

## My Journey: The Power of Love

Three years had passed by since the trial. My car was full of garlands and Christmas lights for the trees outside; I was preparing to "deck the halls." Three weeks earlier, I had collapsed on the floor in tears and finally surrendered to the inner nudging of the *Teacher* to write Eve a letter. In the five-page letter, I was inviting her to begin again, to heal our fractured relationship. I was finally ready to let go of the past.

I had not written the letter to get the girls back—I had written it to complete whatever contracts Eve's and my soul had. I practiced the *A Course in Miracles* teachings, which state that the children of God deserve our gratitude and love, and I gave Eve both.

She sent back an 18-page letter. I devoured her every word, searching for confirmation that she was, in fact, willing to begin again. With that letter, I found a door opening to the possibility that we could finally heal our tattered relationship.

Following my repeated reading of the letter, I turned to the Course and asked for guidance. As I had done countless times before, I just opened the text to whatever page the *Teacher* wanted me to read. My eyes fell upon the following passage:

"You are your brother's savior. He is yours. Reason speaks happily indeed of this. This gracious plan was given love by Love. And what Love plans is like Itself in this: Being united, It would have you learn what you must be. And being one with It, it must be given you to give what It has given, and gives still. Spend but an instant in the glad acceptance of what is given you to give your brother, and learn with him what has been given both of you. To give is no more blessed than to receive. But neither is it less."

When Allan came home that evening, I told him, with tears rolling down my face, what I had done. He cried, too, and urged me to go slowly and carefully. I promised I would.

The next morning, I wrote Eve another letter. The question is, "Is there anything love will not heal?" In that moment, I knew with every cell of my being — and have never forgotten since — that the answer is NO.

## My Journey Continued: A Second Chance

Eve and I wrote back and forth for a while, and eventually, the girls began writing, too. Tasha was initially the most interested in resuming a relationship. She was quick to acknowledge that the only way I could get to her and her sisters was through Eve.

About a month after my letter of invitation to heal and start over, Eve and I went for lunch together. The event was somewhat like our long meeting 14 years earlier in the Boston Pizza in Lethbridge. The dramatic difference was that this was a meeting marking a blending together, not a tearing apart. If, in fact, we are certain to always experience both sides of love, which I believe to be true, then this was the other side for Eve and me. We talked from 12 noon until 6 P.M., discussing *A Course in Miracles* and the children's lives during the time that I did not have access to them. Afterwards, Eve invited me to her home to see the girls.

Seeing my girls again after such a long time felt surreal. Hugs and warmth streamed from my heart; my daughters seemed reserved, and unconvinced this would last. From my standpoint, we were on the road to new beginnings.

## I Hurt You—I Am Sorry

When we are getting divorced, it goes without question that we have hurt, and been hurt by, our former spouse. It can be a powerful healing agent to make a list of the things for which you can take personal responsibility in the deterioration of the marriage. I am a firm believer in the idea that whenever a marriage ends, it is both individuals who have contributed to its completion. Every action and behavior we receive from our spouse, be it positive or negative, has something to do with us. The most constructive question we can ask ourselves is, What have I done to contribute to this person's behavior towards me? This is the deeper questioning of an emotionally mature person. Conversely, emotionally young adults believe that they are innocent victims of their spouse's destructive or selfish behaviors. They believe that the marriage breakdown is primarily the other person's fault. Both these beliefs are untrue, and will perpetuate hostility between the couple in the upcoming years. If the couple has the lifelong task of raising children together, such crippling mindsets will hurt their kids.

Each person must find the wisdom and honesty within themselves to admit the mistakes, behaviors, mindsets, and words that have hurt the other. To do so allows each person to move forward, and to advance the healing of their hearts and minds, so that they can communicate more effectively in the future.

Unaddressed and unadmitted, past hurtful actions and words leave wounds which infect our future. These hurts contaminate all our upcoming interactions. They create unclean emotions that seep through our words. The seepage becomes infectious and spreads.

To say to our former life partner that we are sorry for the pain we have brought them and for the lost dream of a life we once committed to creating is transformative, and it sets a stage for a more caring relationship. Further, these words can foster actions that enable both people to move forward and aid them in building new trust and hope with one another, to create a new friendship based on respect.

## My Journey: Purging the Soul

In a moment of sanity or desperation—I am not sure what inspired her—Eve finally confessed the story of our past. She said she trusted that no matter what she had said or done, we would all love her. She wanted to confess all the cruel things she had done all of those years. She sat with each of the girls and shared what she had really done and felt. She cleansed her soul, her heart and mind, and they just listened. She told them that she had been terrified of their loving me more than her—terrified that one day they would leave, and that she was "not good enough" as a mom.

The girls were not surprised by Eve's confession because somewhere in their hearts, they had known this all along. She finally admitted that I had never abandoned them. She had lied about the aggravated assault and other incidents. Meanwhile, Adam denied everything she confessed to. She was now trapped between two worlds, and only one way out would save her.

By late October, Tasha was starting to see the manipulative and controlling nature of Adam and Eve. She could not believe that she had been so blind. I reminded her that they were still being driven by fear.

A week later, Adam called to tell me that his van engine was gone. The van had been Adam and Eve's only remaining form of transportation, and he could not afford to get it repaired. I offered to pay for the repair, and he could pay me back later. He accepted, and we carried on. A month later, I suggested that the easiest way for Adam and Eve to repay the $5,000 loan was for me to suspend child support payments until it was paid off. They reluctantly agreed. They had hoped that, since Allan and I were financially comfortable, we would just "gift" the loan. Allan and I had discussed this option, but decided that we did not owe them anything, and we were already contributing to the girls' physical needs in the way of cash and clothing.

Interestingly, since I had returned into Adam and Eve's life, they had had a long string of mishaps, including a car accident; transmission problems in Adam's jeep, which they could also not afford to get repaired; health issues; and finally the van engine, which was the most costly. It was as if the cosmos were saying, "It's time to tell the truth about the past."

One October evening, I received a call from Tasha. She was sobbing hysterically. Her relationship with Adam and Eve had become seriously strained because she refused to allow them to continue intimidating her. There was verbal abuse, and eventually a physical fight. I knew from what I had witnessed on the driveway three years earlier what their fights looked and sounded like. Tasha told me that, at one point in this fight, Adam had her pinned against the wall, holding her by the throat. She kicked him off and ran to her room. Finally, she found the strength to stand up to him, and in her heart, she decided then that she would move out.

During the next month, she became reclusive. Adam and Eve suspected that she was planning a move. This infuriated them, and tensions mounted.

By December, Tasha could no longer bear living there. She often remarked about Eve's sarcastic comments about me. Eve was becoming increasingly jealous. She told both Emma and Tasha that I had staged the whole year of appearing so caring, just to get them back. Both girls began to see more and more clearly the distortions of Eve's thinking. Sara remained oblivious to it all.

Emma and Tasha always said that there had been enormous favoritism in their house because Adam and Eve's son and Sara were allowed to live by a whole different set of rules.

Emma, who would be graduating from high school the following May, had also recently announced her intention to move out right after her graduation. Both Tasha and Emma were no longer willing to endure the disabling control and emotional manipulation to which they had been subjected. Adam and Eve's control over the girls' decision-making processes was fading; they were reverting to their old ways of intimidation and fear to get the children to comply.

## My Journey Continued: Tasha Comes Home

Tasha called me at the office one day—she was hysterical, crying, and asking me to pick her up right away. I called Allan, who was on his way home, and asked him to pick her up. Allan arrived at Adam and Eve's house to find Tasha terrified that Adam or Eve would come home before she could get away.

Later, Tasha explained the unfoldment of the events leading to this outcome. She said she had asked for a family meeting to discuss her wish to move out. Then, that day after school, she had found

Eve sobbing at the kitchen table and asked her why she was crying. Eve answered that she had done her best, but that now it was "time to go." Eve said, "You now have Moreah and no longer need me. I left a note for your father." Tasha became frightened and asked what Eve was talking about. She had long realized that this was the way that Eve controlled the family. She often threatened to leave when she was not feeling appreciated or validated. She then questioned Tasha about whether she was planning to move in with me, and Tasha admitted that she did want to try this to see how it would feel. Eve became hysterical and left. Tasha ran upstairs, called me, and stuffed everything she wanted to take into garbage bags. She was terrified that Adam would come home before she was gone.

An hour a later, Adam called. He was furious and unreasonable with me. He again said that he would find a way to get back at me, and end my relationship with the girls. I hung up the phone, knowing in my heart that my dance with him was over!

The girls, Emma and Tasha, would attempt one more time to patch things up, but that attempt, too, would fail because of Adam and Eve's continued dishonesty about past events and their desire to remove me from the children's lives. A year later, Emma moved in with us, too.

In the fall of 2002, Adam left Eve, taking Sara with him. A year later, he told Eve that he wanted a divorce.

Currently, Sara and I are not speaking, but I pray that in time, a bridge will be constructed on which we can meet. Sara occasionally speaks with and sees Emma and Emma's son, but has not yet reconciled the truth with Tasha. Tasha remains clear that until Sara wants the real truth about what happened, she is unavailable for a sister relationship.

## Journal Exercise:

Please answer the following question on page 132 in your *New Divorce Paradigm Journal*:

- What apologies need to be made?

# Staying in the Day

In as many ways as a divorce is an ending, it is also a beginning. It offers you an opportunity to "clean house," to revisit yourself and make positive changes, and to increase your personal standards. It is a time to reflect on all that you loved in your past and wish to recreate. It is also a time to look upon what was in need of change or correction, and to make those improvements.

It is natural to be afraid and apprehensive about the many decisions that lie ahead. A mistake commonly made by divorcing individuals is to think that everything must start happening at once. It will not, nor could all your decisions be made in a single day. Think of your divorce process as the building of a skyscraper. First comes the surveying and then the architecture. Next is the building of a firm foundation. Then come the steel, concrete, and interior footprint layout. Finally, the finishing work is done, and then you have a building. This process often takes three years to complete, and it may take you three years to completely heal from a divorce also.

What is of critical importance while going through a divorce is the attitude with which you proceed. It is highly recommended to get your financial house in order first, so have your assets assessed by a qualified accountant and financial planner before any division of property begins.

Next, come to an agreement with your spouse regarding the parenting plan. It is important that you do not treat your children like possessions. Give them the same stability in divorce that they had during the marriage. Choose a primary house that the children can call "base camp," even though they will have two homes. Children need to feel rooted, so one of the two homes needs to feel like the primary residence. Think about how you would feel to be constantly moving between two homes. Kids are resilient, but it is best if they are allowed to feel rooted in a primary home. If this is not a possibility for you, then be sure that there is a kind and caring relationship between you and your former spouse. Kids do best when they feel that their parents still care about each other.

After the assessment of your assets and liabilities is complete, start negotiating the fair division of the assets and liabilities. Again, remember to consider what is fair for all.

Emotional healing will occur in the months and years following the divorce. Some people take as much as five years to recover from the wounds and lost dream of a life they had envisioned, while others move on quickly—sometimes too quickly, leaving shards and bruises hidden beneath the surface, which will be exposed through the future relationships they envelop. Most of all, be patient and kind to yourself as you transition.

My last suggestion, if you are going through a divorce, is to find a skilled divorce coach or therapist who can guide your progress and act as a sounding board with respect to the many decisions that lie ahead for you.

Spiritually speaking, the transition of divorce is certain to facilitate soul growth and inspire a deeper understanding of self. Prayer and meditation are powerful support tools during this fragile time in your life, so don't be afraid to ask for, and expect, miracles!

Now that you have completed reading this book and begun the healing and growth process through working with the accompanying *New Divorce Paradigm Journal*, you are well equipped for proceeding on your sacred journey. Remember you are not alone; within you is a wise and trustworthy companion and Teacher!

Every end is a new beginning.

Author unknown

# About the Author

Moreah Ragusa, RFM, is a psychotherapist, registered family mediator, marriage counselor, corporate coach, and a popular speaker and seminar leader. She has been a student and teacher of the internationally acclaimed spiritual text *A Course in Miracles* for more than fifteen years and is recognized for her ability to illuminate and clarify its teachings.

Deeply committed to helping others on their life path, Moreah is the founder and president of the Phoenix Coaching and Transformation Corporation in Calgary, Alberta. The company offers life mastery strategies to reveal each individual's inherent wisdom, prosperity, freedom, and power.

Moreah is the author of *The New Marriage Paradigm: Inspiring the Transformation and Evolution of Committed Relationships* and two previous books on spiritual transformation. The first, *Rediscovering Your Authentic Self*, based on *A Course in Miracles*, has helped many to understand the connection of thought and experience. The second, *Our Cosmic Dance*, is a candid autobiography offered as a teaching model for personal and relationship growth.

Passionate about sharing her deep understanding of spiritual truths and the human journey, Moreah has appeared on numerous radio and television shows.

# Other Books by Moreah Ragusa

- **Rediscovering Your Authentic Self:**
  Applying A Course in Miracles to Everyday Life
  Also available on CD in audio book format; abridged
- **Our Cosmic Dance:**
  An Autobiography of Courage, Faith, and Spiritual
  Triumph
- **The New Marriage Paradigm:**
  Inspiring the Transformation and Evolution of
  Committed Relationships

## Journals:

- **The New Divorce Paradigm Journal:**
  An Explorative Workbook Designed to Support Your
  Journey to Marriage Completion
- **The New Marriage Paradigm Journal:**
  An Explorative Workbook Designed to Strengthen
  Your Committed Relationship

## CDs:

- **Relationships: Our Journey to Enlightenment**
  Recording of a live lecture series on relationships
- **Understanding A Course in Miracles**
  Recording of a live lecture series, discussing the
  meaning of various topics explored in *A Course in
  Miracles*, including love, forgiveness, guilt, and
  atonement
- **Creating Mastery in Your Life**
  Recording of a live lecture series, discussing topics
  such as how to apply the laws of love to different
  areas of your life, including the areas of money,
  relationships, and health

## Contact Information

To order Moreah's books and CDs, for information on our services, or to book Moreah for a lecture, conference, seminar, or retreat, please visit our

Web site:   www.thephoenixcoaching.com

             info@thephoenixcoaching.com

Or call:    403-278-3700